"Pete Hise's passion to help you achieve th
put inside you is evident from the very firs
Are You Waiting For? The wisdom of his lif
engaging nature of his personal stories will
confidently into the future God always inte........... ... .

STEVEN FURTICK
Lead pastor, Elevation Church; author of the *New York Times*
bestseller *Greater*

"As an evangelist and abolitionist, I firmly believe one of the best
questions is: 'What life are you waiting for?' Too many times we
are halted by fear or apathy, when we should really be rising to
the occasion and living the life we were intended to live. I love
Pete's passion to seize the moment and experience the fullness
God desires for us. So seize the moment and start reading this
book NOW!"

CHRISTINE CAINE
Founder of The A21 Campaign and bestselling author of *Undaunted*

"I'm a big believer and living proof of the idea that God is not only
a *Giver* of big dreams, but also a *Provider* of the stuff to help us
reach those dreams. My good friend Pete Hise has inspired us once
again to keep pushing toward following and believing in God to
help us achieve those dreams. "

MAC POWELL
Lead singer of Third Day and solo country artist

"One of the things I fear most in my own life is getting to the end
of it, looking back, and seeing all of the things I wished I would
have done. In this book Pete destroys the idea that continually
saying 'someday' will enable us to accomplish immeasurably more
than all we could ever ask or imagine. I heard someone say once
that 'someday is a disease that will take your dreams to the grave

with you.' Reading this book will put an exclamation point on that statement and encourage you to step out in faith and really dive into what Jesus has called you to do."

PERRY NOBLE
Senior pastor, NewSpring Church; author of *Unleash!* and *Overwhelmed*

"If you feel held back and overpowered by *maybe someday* thoughts like, 'Maybe someday I'll live a fuller life, maybe someday I'll get the big break, maybe someday I'll start pursuing my calling,' then you've got to read this book. You don't have to wait for someday. You don't have to stand on the sidelines. This book will guide you through life-transforming principles that will lead you on a courageous journey to grab a hold of who God has called you to be and live the life you were made for."

PETE WILSON
Pastor of Cross Point Church and author of *Plan B* and *Let Hope In*

"Pete Hise is one of a kind. Not only is Pete a passionate pastor, he is a superb leader. When I've preached at Quest Community Church, it has been nothing short of miraculous. They have created a culture of redemption under his leadership, and they care deeply about helping people meet Jesus and walk with Him as Lord and Savior. When you read *What Life Are You Waiting For?* it's like you are having coffee with Pete. This book is a tour of the heart of a pastor who wants God's best for everyone he comes in contact with. The message is simple. Stop waiting and wishing. Start believing God and becoming who He wants you to be. This book is simple yet profound, convicting yet encouraging, and filled with motivational rocket fuel! Get a copy for yourself and everyone you love, because it has the potential to set things in motion that can change the outcome of your life, and your world, for the glory of God!"

DR. CLAYTON KING
President, Crossroads Ministries; teaching pastor, NewSpring Church; Distinguished Professor of Evangelism, Anderson University

"I love it when people write about what they actually live. Pete Hise is on a quest to create a world without regret—where all of us live the life we were created to live."

ERWIN RAPHAEL McMANUS
Pastor, Mosaic Church; author of *The Barbarian Way* and
Chasing Daylight

"Pete Hise is inspiring and infectious! His belief in the life-changing power of God will compel you and challenge you to take the transformational adventure that he believes God has called you to. *What Life Are You Waiting For?* will push you to ask tough questions, grapple with unresolved heart issues and, most importantly, compel you to 'push play.'"

JENNI CATRON
Church leader and author of *Clout*

"The first time I encountered Pete Hise, my soul was tattooed by this inspiring reality: This man passionately loves Jesus, the Gospel, and people. When you read *What Life Are You Waiting For?* your soul will be tattooed too. You will love Jesus, the Gospel, and people more. Get ready for the adventurous life that awaits you."

DERWIN L. GRAY
Lead pastor, Transformation Church; author of *Limitless Life*

"God has given Pete a unique ability to inspire us and give us hope for change. This work not only does that—it tells us how! A must-read!"

SHAWN LOVEJOY
Lead pastor, Mountain Lake Church; author of *The Measure of Our Success*

"With scintillating stories and remarkable spiritual insight, Pete Hise puts together a first-class manual for crashing through life's limits. Live large now. What life are you waiting for?"

MARK ASHTON
Lead pastor, Christ Community Church (Omaha, Nebraska)

"Smart, funny, and challenging, *What Life Are You Waiting For?* will reignite your dreams as Pete Hise invites you on a transformational journey of discovering your full potential in Christ. Through biblical teaching and compelling stories of real life change, Pete shows us how we can do more than just observe life—we can truly live it the way God intended."

TONY MORGAN
Consultant, leadership coach, author (TonyMorganLive.com)

"What we have here is a modern-day story of a God who is interested in us being a part of His purpose for the world by inviting people to take a radical step, and an ordinary guy who said, 'Count me in!' Sounds so simple, but it's not! Pete lets us walk in his shoes as he wrestled with what his next step might be. The miracle was that he took it, a church was birthed, and a generation is hearing about the God who asked him to take the step in the first place—Jesus! So, what if you took a step?"

DAVID SMITH
Lead pastor, Fairhaven Church (Centerville, Ohio)

"Have you ever read a book and asked yourself, 'How did the author know my life, my questions, my challenges?' This is one of *those* books. When you open the pages of *What Life Are You Waiting For?* you won't just be reading words—you'll find yourself responding to them personally. I'm grateful for a road map that leads to the life I've been waiting for!"

HELEN MUSICK
Transformation Pastor, Quest Community Church; coauthor of *Everyday Object Lessons for Youth Groups*

WHAT
LIFE
ARE YOU
WAITING
FOR?

Push Play on the Adventure
God Has for You

For Eric

PETE HISE

Push Play Now!

**TYNDALE
MOMENTUM**

Pete Hise

Eph. 3:16-19

An Imprint of
Tyndale House Publishers, Inc.

Visit Tyndale online at www.tyndale.com.

Visit Tyndale Momentum online at www.tyndalemomentum.com.

TYNDALE is a registered trademark of Tyndale House Publishers, Inc. *Tyndale Momentum* and the Tyndale Momentum logo are trademarks of Tyndale House Publishers, Inc. Tyndale Momentum is an imprint of Tyndale House Publishers, Inc.

What Life Are You Waiting For?: Push Play on the Adventure God Has for You

Designed by Daniel Farrell

Published in association with the literary agency of Yates & Yates (www.yates2.com).

Unless otherwise indicated, all Scripture quotations are taken from the *Holy Bible,* New Living Translation, copyright © 1996, 2004, 2007, 2013 by Tyndale House Foundation. (Some quotations may be from the NLT1, copyright © 1996.) Used by permission of Tyndale House Publishers, Inc., Carol Stream, Illinois 60188. All rights reserved.

Scripture quotations marked NIV are taken from the Holy Bible, *New International Version,*® *NIV.*® Copyright © 1973, 1978, 1984, 2011 by Biblica, Inc.® (Some quotations may be from the earlier NIV edition, copyright © 1984.) Used by permission of Zondervan. All rights reserved worldwide. www.zondervan.com.

Scripture quotations marked *The Message* are taken from *The Message* by Eugene H. Peterson, copyright © 1993, 1994, 1995, 1996, 2000, 2001, 2002. Used by permission of NavPress Publishing Group. All rights reserved.

Scripture quotations marked TLB are taken from *The Living Bible*, copyright © 1971 by Tyndale House Foundation. Used by permission of Tyndale House Publishers, Inc., Carol Stream, Illinois 60188. All rights reserved.

Scripture quotations marked AMP are taken from the *Amplified Bible,*® copyright © 1954, 1958, 1962, 1964, 1965, 1987 by The Lockman Foundation. Used by permission.

Library of Congress Cataloging-in-Publication Data

Hise, Pete.
   What life are you waiting for?: push play on the adventure God has for you/Pete Hise.
     pages cm
   ISBN 978-1-4143-8676-8 (sc)
   1. Christian life. I. Title.
   BV4501.3.H59 2014
   248.4—dc23   2013049740

Printed in the United States of America

20	19	18	17	16	15	14
8	7	6	5	4	3	2

To the church I didn't think still existed . . .

Thank you, Quest Community, for being living proof
that God still builds loving cultures of redemption.

You are contagious.
You are irresistible.
You are irrefutable evidence that
everyone who runs to Him makes it!

Thank you for letting me fill these pages with your stories.
You led me to fall head over heels in love with the Church.

I love you with my whole heart.
Our best days are still before us!

CONTENTS

FOREWORD

PETE HISE is a force of nature. I have rarely met a more determined man! Which makes me very grateful that he is a dedicated Christ-follower and a fantastic pastor. All of that energy is focused in a God-honoring direction!

I first met Pete after a Willow Creek Leadership Conference. He told me, in a most sincere way, that God had prompted him to start a church. I wished him well. Imagine my surprise a few years later when Pete invited me to come to Quest Community Church and help inspire his congregation to make sacrificial financial gifts so that they could purchase a plot of land and build a permanent home. I will never forget that night. Ten members of his new church stood before an overflow crowd and bore witness to the transforming love of Christ. Such sincerity. So many tears. Flying home that night, I had a sense that God had great things in store for that upstart church.

In 2009 I was invited back to Quest and received the grand tour of their sixteen-acre campus and glistening new buildings. My heart overflowed with a fatherly kind of pride in Pete and his staff. Their church had far exceeded my expectations.

In coming years you will hear a lot more about Pete Hise and Quest Community Church. I have the feeling he has just laid the foundation for what is going to become a powerful movement for Christ for many years to come. I will be cheering him on from Chicago.

Bill Hybels
December 2013

Chapter 1

WHAT IF?

THE WHOLE CROWD JUMPED to their feet as the wide receiver reversed direction and came flying around the near corner with the football tucked under his right arm. In a full-out sprint he rushed down the field with the entire defense chasing him. Passing the fifty, the forty, the thirty, the twenty, he kept running until only one man had a legitimate shot at tackling him. At the ten-yard line, the defender dove for the wide receiver's feet—and missed. *Touchdown!* An exhilarating fourth-quarter TD for the speedster . . . the first of his career.

After the football game ended, I had a chance to speak with the star receiver who'd just made the game-winning touchdown. He was willing to give me a brief interview because it turns out that number eight, the rookie wide receiver, is my youngest son, Carson. It was his first year of football, and I went out of my mind when he scored. To my surprise, Carson was pretty cool about the whole experience. As we stood on the sideline after the game, I talked and talked about his scoring play; he drank Gatorade. When I stopped talking and he paused gulping, my eight-year-old asked me a very serious question:

"Dad, do you think I'll be picked *first* in the NFL draft?"

In my opinion, he could have asked any number of questions that seemed more appropriate: "Do you think I'll ever score a *second* touchdown?" "Will I be good enough to play in high school?" "Do you think I'll get the chance to play college ball?" or even "Do you think I'll ever be forty-eight inches tall?"

But he didn't. With one TD behind him, Carson asked with absolute seriousness, "Do you think I'll be taken *first* in the NFL draft?"

There he stood, all fifty-eight pounds of him, with sweaty curls sticking out of his helmet, never doubting for a second that he'd be drafted by the pros someday. He just wondered if he'd be taken first.

Somewhere along the way, we've all had NFL-size dreams. Can you remember yours? Most of us can't, because we didn't have them for very long. We dreamed big when we were young, but as we grew older, our grand dreams shifted. Instead of becoming an NFL player, the president of the United States like our parents told us we'd be, or the astronaut our grandparents dreamed we'd be, we started to settle. Eventually, we settled for the "real world": studying for exams, changing diapers, sitting through job reviews, chauffeuring our kids around town, paying bills. Somewhere between elementary school and where we are right now, we traded what *might be* for what *is*.

WE SELL OURSELVES SHORT

Smart money would suggest that when you opened this book and began reading, you probably didn't expect very much from God. Certainly nothing that would fall into the "amazing" category—it's a *book* after all, right? It's not like you're stepping into a pivotal meeting, receiving an offer, or considering a proposal that could change your life. You are just reading a book.

But what if God has more in mind for you as you make your way through these pages?

What if?

As a pastor, I have the privilege of connecting with lots of different people—people like you and me—each with a unique background and story. Frequently our encounters deal with the idea of change. More specifically, we often discuss life change, real transformation. When the idea of a divine "what if" is raised, most people tend to believe that God has the power to transform a human life; they just don't expect that He will do it in *them*.

Here's the typical train of thought: "Is it possible that God might do something important in some people's lives? Sure, it's possible. But not in me. I'm too ordinary, too flawed. I doubt God would use someone like me to do anything that really matters."

I want to challenge your low expectations of God and compel you to recapture the innocence of your youth, when you may have daydreamed about the great plans of God for your life. Entertain the reality that God has more in store for you than you know. No matter where you come from or what's going on in your life, I hope you'll consider the possibility that you will encounter Him in a very real way through these pages.

A CRACK IN THE DOOR

The Bible says that God knew every single day of your life before one of them came to pass. What if that is really true? That means He saw this moment coming a long time ago, well before you could even read one of these words. In fact, Psalm 139:15 says that He saw you in your mother's womb. He saw that moment with the same clarity He sees *this* moment. If God is who the Bible says He is—limitless in power, bound by neither time nor space—then that's no big stretch.

> What if God wants to impact your today so that it changes your tomorrow?

So humor me. Entertain that "what if" for a moment. What if God orchestrated this moment so He could inject the possibility that He wants to do something substantial in *your* life? What if God wants to impact your today so that it changes your tomorrow?

It's a beautiful premise, isn't it? In the mind and heart of God, you are not an accident. Therefore, maybe you should at least be open to the possibility that God might have something more in mind for you.

I'm banking on it.

Long before I ever typed a single word of this book, I began praying for you. I don't necessarily know your name, but I've prayed that your heart would be open, ready, and available to encounter God Himself.

Here's why: God doesn't need much help.

Do you know what God needs in order to do something phenomenal in your life?

A crack in the door.

A pinch of possibility.

Even the smallest seed of hope.

Most people miss that simple truth and resign themselves to living life as if God can't do much to change things. But here and now, understand once and for all the heart of God: *If you give Me the tiniest margin, I will do something in you that will take your breath away. I have a heart that cares, and I have the power to act in your life so that things are different tomorrow from how they are today.*

> Do you know what God needs in order to do something phenomenal in your life? A crack in the door.

God wants to ignite His power in your life to transform

you. He is very interested in the timeline of that change because He wants it to occur *now*—a watershed event that causes a ripple effect through the rest of your days and years.

FIRSTHAND EVIDENCE

I am not asserting this from secondhand stories, hearsay, and rumors. I have experienced firsthand the power of God to instantaneously change a human life forever—mine. It's like I want to scream for all to hear, "Paul is telling the truth!" when he writes in Ephesians,

> It's in Christ that we find out who we are and what we are living for. Long before we first heard of Christ and got our hopes up, he had his eye on us, had designs on us for glorious living, part of the overall purpose he is working out in everything and everyone. EPHESIANS 1:11, *THE MESSAGE*

On a snowy night in upstate New York, I was sitting in a church listening to four men in blue leisure suits sing about Jesus, while I harbored thoughts of how much I wanted to kill the friend of mine who had suckered me into being there. There was no forewarning to tip me off about what was going to happen in me before I left.

From a young age, I was constantly in trouble. In fifth grade I had pushed my teacher, Ms. Tulloch, so far over the edge that she had developed a behavioral conduct system that involved a sheet of paper on the corner of my desk. Every time I got in trouble, she would add a little check mark. The warning was clear: ten marks equaled a parent-teacher conference. She was trying to offer me a fresh start, a chance to begin again.

At the end of the first day, I had thirty-five check marks on that paper.

By the time I was fifteen, I was much older than fifteen. The trouble I was getting into was no longer triggering parent-teacher conferences; it was steering my life toward a darkening trajectory. I viewed women as objects, valued people only as they benefited me, and hung out with friends who aided and abetted my downward spiral.

So when a buddy lured me into that church on November 12, 1982, under the auspices of "attending a concert," I was furious and freaked out when I realized I was going to hear Christian music. Trapped in the middle of a row, unable to escape, I was forced to endure the four-part gospel harmonies to the bitter end.

As the concert wrapped up, one of the blue-suited men with a mustache stepped forward and started talking to the crowd about Jesus, the Person they had been singing about. He told us of how Jesus had left heaven on an all-out search-and-rescue mission for every person in the world; that He chose death on the cross to forgive our sins, change our hearts, and give us a brand-new start. Except what I heard was "to forgive *your* sins, change *your* heart, and give *you* a brand-new start."

"Somebody here tonight is in need of a second chance.

You've made a mess of your life and think you've gone too far, but you haven't. If you surrender your life to Jesus, He will take it and receive you—He will give your life a fresh start." *How did that man know? I'd never even met him before.*

My heart started pounding in my chest: *Is anyone else listening to this?* I looked around the room. The offer couldn't have been any clearer—and it felt like the deal of a lifetime. The God of the Universe loved me, had made a way for me to be forgiven of my considerable rap sheet through the Cross, and wanted to come lead my life out of brokenness into a whole new God-made plan. How could I possibly pass it up?

Before I knew what was happening, I hit the aisle and headed toward the man with the mustache at the front of the church. To this day, I don't know if I was the only one. I just knew that I wasn't going to miss my moment. I walked quickly, sure that someone was going to recognize me and say "Not you, Pete. This isn't for people like you." But no one did. I made it there safely, and with my head bowed I prayed from the bottom of my heart and asked Jesus to forgive me, to come into my heart, and to lead my life. My heart exploded with the reality of His forgiveness and love.

I left that church a brand-new man! My friend, and those who knew me, were stunned. When they asked why I went down front, I explained that I felt my heart beating out of my chest . . . like the man was speaking directly to me.

Lying in bed that night, I alternated between laughter

and tears. *It is all true. Jesus is true to His word.* I could *feel* the difference immediately: my thoughts were different, my emotions were different, and more than anything, I wanted to tell everyone I knew. I felt like I had been given the cure to a spiritual cancer that had been eating away at my heart my whole life. I had no idea if anyone knew that Jesus was this real, this available, or this able to transform their hearts and lives—but I knew that I would spend the rest of my life telling everyone I could.

ENDING THE CYCLE

When you hear the word *change*, what comes to mind? Maybe you think about it in terms of resolutions or setting goals, trying to positively manage the cycle of wishing and waiting. You know the cycle, right? *Wishing* our circumstances would change and *waiting* for it to happen to us. After all, many of us live as though life owes us something and fate will cause it to come our way if we just wish and wait long enough.

That's not the kind of change I'm talking about.

The kind of transformation that God has in mind has nothing to do with passively waiting. Living life on pause—and neglecting to take action—while thinking that breakthrough change is on the way is just a delusion. Nothing important in life works that way.

Think about it. The unemployed dude who never lifts a finger to type up a résumé or fill out an application, who's just waiting for some company to hear of his legendary skills and offer a job out of the blue doesn't end up employed. He becomes that guy living in his mom's basement, guzzling Mountain Dew and perfecting his Xbox technique.

The woman who yearns for a group of real friends to do life with but who never chooses to position herself in community with others or take the risk of getting to know new people just becomes that lady with the house full of cats, each named after a celebrity.

Simply put, if you don't take action, nothing changes.

> You can't rewind or replay your life. You get one shot.

And that's what this book is about. It is a cry for the end of the cycle of wishing and waiting. The truth is that you and I don't have nine lives to spend waiting for something to change. I don't mean to sound morbid, but the reality is that you won't get another shot, my friend. You can't rewind or replay your life. You get one shot. What life are you waiting for?

In the early days of our church, Richard, a man in his late sixties, attended often. He enjoyed church, but make no mistake, he was there on his own terms. He hadn't bought into this Christianity thing yet. We'd stay late after services talking through his questions about faith, and after every talk, he'd walk away, saying, "I'm not ready yet, but maybe someday."

That all changed when Richard had a life-threatening heart attack. I remember standing in the emergency room with his family—people we loved—begging God for more time as Richard was speeding toward an eternity he wasn't ready for.

As the medical team strongly urged family and friends to rush their good-byes, God responded to our prayer and gave us exactly what we'd asked for—more time. Later that week Sharon, a pastor at Quest, and I were visiting Richard in the ICU, and we had one of our now-familiar talks about his faith. Only this time, there was a different sobriety and urgency in our talk. Having nearly died just days earlier, Richard was experiencing a newfound level of spiritual clarity. I asked him if he wanted to give his life to Christ, and he said, "I'd like to . . . but I have so many unanswered questions."

I looked at this man, who seemed to have only days to live, and made this suggestion: "Richard, what if you step out in the faith you *do* have and let Jesus answer your questions once He is in your heart, perhaps even in heaven?"

Richard looked up, alert. "I didn't know you could do that!" he said. "I'm ready!"

And with machines beeping all around us, I led Richard in the most important prayer of his life. In a moment of humble surrender, he gave his life to Christ. The joy and peace that filled that hospital room—and Richard's heart— were unmistakable. I've never quite recovered from that last-minute rescue.

You see, just a few weeks later, Richard went to be with Jesus. He'd spent his whole life saying "maybe someday," and at the last possible moment, he received the life he was made for. He only got to experience that freedom and peace on *this* side of eternity for a few weeks, but now he lives it fully with Jesus *face-to-face*.

Here's the deal: *Richard didn't have to wait!* And neither do you.

If God stands available and ready to move, then why wouldn't we go for it and join Him in what could turn out to be something more substantial than we ever imagined?

I could tell you about people, real people. Friends of mine at Quest Community Church that I have the privilege of serving who decided to take action now and believe God; people who have chosen to live out the divine "what if" for their lives. I could tell you about:

- Scott, a successful businessman who traded the emptiness of wealth to serve those in extreme poverty in India.
- Cecily, a former stripper who found redemption in Christ and now helps pastors from across the nation reach people who are far from God.
- John, a thriving football coach who overcame his guilt when he humbled himself and received forgiveness and now lives in awe as all three of his children have followed in his footsteps.
- Craig, a former atheist who is now a church elder helping people find the hope of Christ for themselves.
- Dani, a timid girl from the country who never thought she'd make much of a difference, who left behind the safe, small life she knew. She's now a

woman who's eager to make an impact and influence scores and scores of people.

- Todd, an attorney and former drug addict on the verge of suicide, who now spends his life leading a recovery ministry helping others find sobriety and significance.
- Clay and Rachel, a couple whose marriage was destroyed in the wake of an affair, who now lead a thriving marriage ministry.

The goal, over the course of our journey together, is to invite God to move and then follow Him into a Transformation Adventure; that He would help us overcome the cycle of wishing and waiting, and finally make war against all the things that keep us complacently locked out of being who God created us to be.

IT'S TIME FOR A CULTURE SHIFT

I am a lifelong, die-hard Dallas Cowboys fan. My earliest memories of sports are of cheering on "Captain Comeback" Roger Staubach as he led the 'Boys to one fourth-quarter victory after another.

In recent years my team has not enjoyed the same success as it did in the seventies, eighties, and nineties. In fact, since the glory days of Emmitt Smith, Michael Irvin, and Troy Aikman, Dallas has been extremely mediocre. (You have no idea how painful it is to type that sentence.) My oldest son,

Corey, recently reminded me that during his lifetime, our team (yes, I'm raising Cowboys fans) has won only *one* play-off game. One!

But here's the reality for every true fan: even after a decade of subpar football, each season begins with the general expectation that the Dallas Cowboys could go all the way to the Super Bowl. Every fall, scores of experts and countless fans (including every male under my roof) discuss how this will be "the year" that America's Team returns to its former glory.

Why? What is it that makes us believe year after year? I think I know. Over the last fifty years the Cowboys have created a *culture of winning*. Regardless of the score or their current record, the Cowboys carry with them the lingering possibility of a comeback, a resurrection, a stunning turn-around resulting in a breathtaking victory.

There are few things in life more compelling than a culture of winning. Just ask people who've barely survived a culture of losing. I remember watching an interview with legendary Detroit Lions running back Barry Sanders. Sanders is one of the best to have ever played the game. In July 1999, to everyone's surprise, he retired from the NFL. His legs were still strong, and he was closing in on Walter Payton's rushing title. So why did he hang up his cleats? He couldn't take it any longer. Not the hits, but the losing! During his thirteen-year career, the Lions only had three winning seasons. Barry walked away, not because he couldn't play, but because he couldn't face one more losing effort. Throughout the entire interview I couldn't get over the look of sadness and disappointment in Sanders's eyes.

What about you?

What do you see in your eyes when you look in the mirror? What have you walked away from? Is a culture of losing keeping you off the field? Have you grown so accustomed in your life to settling for the cycle of wishing and waiting that you're being robbed of your childlike innocence and audacity?

That can change today.

With God's help, you can decide, "I'm not waiting anymore. I'm getting off the merry-go-round of wishing and waiting. I'm going to trust God and step into His new territory for my life. I'm not going to waste my one and only life settling or living neck-deep in a culture of losing. I am not going to wait to take action in some next life that is never going to come. I'm going to dare to dream, to believe that God might indeed have more for me than I can see right now."

If that's you, then let's move out together into a brave new world of action within the Transformation Adventure that God has prepared for your life.

What if there is an NFL-size dream just waiting to be resurrected in you?

GETTING TRACTION

REWIND

Through God's power, you can break the cycle of wishing and waiting and step into your Transformation Adventure.

DOWNLOAD

It's in Christ that we find out who we are and what we are living for. Long before we first heard of Christ and got our hopes up, he had his eye on us, had designs on us for glorious living, part of the overall purpose he is working out in everything and everyone. EPHESIANS 1:11, *THE MESSAGE*

PUSH PLAY

Identify the places that are "on pause" in your life and invite God to give you courage for the journey ahead.

Chapter 2

MAKE WAR

THERE'S SOMETHING you probably need to know about me: I love adventure. The exhilaration, the risk . . . I love it all. In fact, I love adventure so much that I've been known to inject adventure into the lives of the people around me, just as a common courtesy.

A couple of summers ago I found myself on a real-life adventure—I was on my first sabbatical, and as a break from the reading, writing, and studying, I took a month-long journey in the Holy Land. Even if you don't find any spiritual significance in the history and legacy of Israel, you've got to admit that it's a calculated risk for an American Christian to spend significant time alone there, amidst such heated, generational conflict in the Middle East. Despite the risks, I anticipated a powerful spiritual pilgrimage, a rich time of exploration and discovery in the lands that I had studied in the Bible for decades.

What I got was essentially Old Testament Boot Camp.

For a solid month, I hiked. I don't mean a leisurely stroll through a wooded glen, or even a brisk backpacking trip on mountain trails. I mean temperatures that make a chilled water bottle hot in thirty minutes. I mean sand and solid rock—everywhere, all the time. No dirt. No grass. Not even something soft and comfortable like asphalt. I mean eight to ten hours a day, Middle Eastern sun beating down on me, walking on rock for "fun."

Among all the incredible places I visited during the month, one of the most memorable sites was Mitzpe Ramon, a jaw-dropping canyon that unexpectedly cuts through the Israeli landscape. Located about fifty miles from the Gaza Strip, the 2,800-foot overlook at Mitzpe Ramon is nothing short of awe-inspiring. As I stayed nearby that night, I witnessed unexpected explosions in the far distance. Consulting the news, I discovered that Ashkelon, one of the towns I had traveled through that very afternoon, had been bombarded with thirty-three rockets in an attack. (Thankfully no one was injured.) I found myself in the middle of a small skirmish, complete with rockets and aircraft soaring overhead—not an uncommon experience for the area—and it touched very near prayers I had prayed for decades for God to bring peace to this divided land. It was unlike anything I had ever personally experienced, and I felt like I had to share this adventure with someone back home.

All the way around the world in Lexington, Kentucky,

my senior staff was gathered for a meeting to advance the ministry of our church, and I naturally assumed that they wouldn't want to miss out on this newest development in my travels. Pulling out my phone, I decided to text them about the events of the day, including the rocket attacks on the town I had just traveled through. After a thorough explanation of this rather intense and exhilarating scene, this is the reply I received from my friend and colleague, Sharon, who was leading the meeting:

> *Holy smokes! Please be as careful and as dangerous as you were made to be.*

I didn't think that was the most sensitive response in light of my report, so I decided to amp up their sense of adventure with a few creative texts. Some might even say I got caught up in the moment and stepped beyond good sense.

> Me: *Crap! I think the hostel where we're staying just got hit.*
>
> Sharon: *Are you serious??? Are you ok??*
>
> Me: *People are here. Soldiers. I can't tell if they are Palestinian or Israeli.*
>
> Sharon: *Dear Jesus, please give Pastor Pete protection and wisdom. . . .*
>
> Me: *Crap. I can't talk. I have to move/run!*

And then I ceased communications . . . for about ten minutes.

After enjoying the beautiful and active night sky, it occurred to me to text them back and let them in on the joke—that my hostel wasn't actually in danger. But it turned out that my well-intentioned little prank had grown. Back home, staff members, elders, the board of directors, and the prayer teams of our church had been mobilized and in that moment were engaged in deep, fervent prayer for their pastor, who was reportedly caught in a firefight on the Gaza Strip. Although I'm known to joke around a lot, this one had gotten away from me. . . . No one was laughing.

What can I say? I hadn't intended to create such a commotion with my ill-advised kidding, but then again, the increased prayer coverage didn't hurt, given the day's rocket attacks. In the end, we all had a good laugh about everything. It wasn't exactly my plan, but it certainly proved to be an adventure!

IN HIS FOOTSTEPS

When it comes to living a life of adventure, Jesus showed us how it's done. We saw Him crash parties, walk on water, flip tables, bring funerals to life. He laughed with His friends, infuriated His enemies, captivated the crowds, risked it all on the forgotten. The truth is, Jesus never met a moment He didn't seize. He lived life to the fullest in intimacy with the Father, living out the plans designed for Him before the beginning of time.

As He walked this planet, Jesus came face-to-face with people He adored. People with destinies and callings—adventures just waiting for them. And it broke His heart to see them not living the free, full, adventurous lives they were designed for. His heart broke for people who were busy judging and being judged, trying and being tried, hating and being hated. People who were harassed and helpless, like sheep without a shepherd.

> Jesus never met a moment He didn't seize. He lived life to the fullest.

When Jesus observed the damage done in the lives of people He loved—damage caused by sinful, hurtful choices—He refused to sit back and do nothing. And in that place of discontent, He made war.

In Romans 6, the apostle Paul writes,

> We know that our old sinful selves were crucified with Christ so that sin might lose its power in our lives. We are no longer slaves to sin. For when we died with Christ we were set free from the power of sin. . . . Sin is no longer your master, for you no longer live under the requirements of the law. Instead, you live under the freedom of God's grace.
>
> ROMANS 6:6-7, 14

Jesus Himself made war once and for all on sin, death, and the enemy. Conquering them all, He also defeated *our* seemingly magnetic pull to make sinful choices. Verse 14 says, "Sin is no longer your master," implying that at one time sin *was* your master.

Every person ever born on earth is born with a sinful nature. Despite how cute a one- or two-year-old is, it only takes spending a couple of hours with one to make this theological observation: "That kid is a little sinner!"

The sad story of our lives is that we are born into a life bullied by sin. But Jesus died on the cross not only to forgive our sin but also to defeat our sinful nature. He has beaten the bully and freed us from the crushing dominion of sin. If you're in Christ, you're free from it, and God intends for you to experience that freedom and live in it!

WHY THE GAP?

If we are no longer under the power of sin, why does it so often appear that sin is still winning? It's a harsh reality, but just because we believe the incredible truth of salvation doesn't mean that we always live in it. Too often it seems the more you try to live it out, the more you realize that you really can't. Rather than be discouraged, I urge you to consider the basis of our faith: Jesus Himself.

> Jesus died on the cross not only to forgive our sin but also to defeat our sinful nature.

When Jesus was put in a tomb, He was actually *dead*. Dead—as in no pulse, no EEG activity. Yes, stone-cold dead for days—rigor mortis, decomposing tissue and all. Now with that graphic picture in mind, have you ever considered that Jesus was absolutely *incapable* of bringing Himself back to life? The One who raised others to life was helpless to help Himself. He deliberately positioned Himself in utter dependence on God's Power (the Holy Spirit) to raise Him to life again.

Did you catch that?

The Son of God was dependent on the Holy Spirit to do what He could not do for Himself!

That, my friend, is great news for those of us who find ourselves helpless. Romans 8:11 says, "The Spirit of God, who raised Jesus from the dead, lives in you. And just as God raised Christ Jesus from the dead, he will give life to your mortal bodies by this same Spirit living within you."

I don't know what dead places in your life may have you feeling stuck, locked away in a tomb of sorts. Perhaps it's a failing marriage, an uncertain future, a distant child, an elusive sense of purpose, or maybe even a gap in your relationship with God. If you can identify the places in your life that feel flatlined, then you have identified where the Spirit of God is waiting to bring His resurrecting work! God Himself longs to fill you with power that does not come from you, but from Him. You don't have to stay in a borrowed tomb. Just like Jesus left His tomb (only slightly used) because He no longer needed it, God wants to send the dead places in your life packing.

> From now on, *someday* is a cuss word.

And here's the kicker: I don't mean *someday*. I mean *now*!

For us to go a step further, with your permission, I need

to rearrange your vocabulary. From now on, *someday* is a cuss word. It's profanity—a curse word, an expletive . . . whatever you want to call it. If we're going to take the offer of transformation from God seriously, we can't hide behind "maybes" and "somedays."

Do you have any idea how many opportunities, adventures, and dreams have died on the altar of "someday"? Aren't you sick of waiting? Jesus did the business of waiting it out in the tomb, so how about we get to the business of *living* the life He died to give us?

NOT WITHOUT A FIGHT

It's time to make war against everything that stands in the way of taking hold of the transformation that Jesus offers us. The road isn't easy, and the resistance is thick. It's going to take diligence and resolve to push through what stands in your way. Waging war for the life Christ offers you isn't a one-time fight. There are daily skirmishes and regular battles that must be fought on your journey.

> The redemption of your soul takes only a moment; the reclamation of your character takes a lifetime.

Colossians 2:6-7 reads, "Just as you accepted Christ Jesus as your Lord, you must continue to follow him. Let your roots grow down into him, and let your lives be built on him."

Jesus died a slow death for us, enabling us to be completely forgiven in an instant by putting our faith and trust in Him. And while the redemption of your soul takes only a moment, the reclamation of your character takes a lifetime. A rescued life is one being rebuilt, day by day, into the image of Jesus. *That* is freedom—a life where sin is no longer your master and you're free to join Him and participate with God as He changes you from the inside out.

But it won't come without a fight.

So as we get started, I want to offer you the best weapons I can. In fact, they don't come from me at all—they are gifts from God. Simple truths that can be the difference between progress and retreat, victory and defeat, life and death. Remember, all He needs is a crack in the door to ignite your destiny, to see His plans being loosed into your life. It's the deal of a lifetime: He provides the power; we provide the agreement. Here are your three keys to traction, tools that will enable you to make war as we begin this Transformation Adventure.

> He provides the power; we provide the agreement.

A DIVINE APPOINTMENT

I was sitting in a leadership conference at Willow Creek Community Church outside Chicago in 1997. I was on a church staff, really loving my job, attending this conference in hopes of finding new tools and a compelling vision to advance our ministry. Willow Creek's senior pastor, Bill Hybels, implored us (the church leaders assembled) to say yes to God, to make our lives count for Him. I'll never forget Bill's urgency as he painted the picture of us standing before God one day. One of the only things that will matter on that day—and for all eternity—is that we did what God asked of us. I still remember his tone, the look on his face, the intensity of his voice as he said, "I challenge you to say yes!"

When Bill threw out that challenge, the most unexpected thing began taking place in my heart. Even though there were thousands of people around me, I felt like I was the only person in the room. God was speaking directly to me, and the message was undeniable: *I want you to quit your job and start a church.* Three seconds later (with my mouth still hanging open), I distinctly recall responding in my mind, *I'm going to quit my job and go start a church.* It wasn't up for discussion—it was from God, and it was already a done deal in my heart. For the rest of the leadership session, I joyfully dove into agreement with God's marching orders for my life, as unbelievable as they were. *I'm about to resign from the job that sent me here to this conference.* One whisper from God changed everything.

INSTANT YES

I don't believe that whispers from God are in short supply. I believe that He has challenges and adventures waiting for us all the time. But He won't force them on us. The key that opens the door to transformation is *our response.*

If you want to see God's power unleashed in your life,

your most effective path begins with an *instant yes*. No matter what He says—no arguing, no delaying, no committee meetings. For those who would make war, the battle cry is "Yes, God!" in advance.

> The key that opens the door to transformation is *our response*.

So what is God whispering to you today? Maybe you heard it as you left for work this morning, as you considered the people and challenges on your prayer list, as you've been reading this book. What if you gave God your instant agreement?

Yes, God.
I will make the phone call.
I will forgive that person.
I will admit the truth.
I will write that check.
I will talk to my neighbor.
I will humble myself.
I will love my spouse.
I will lead these kids.
I will be at church this weekend.
I will tell someone about You.
I will meet You in the mornings.
Yes. Yes. Yes. Instantly—no hesitation.

IMMEDIATE ACTION

Saying an instant yes sets the stage for God's transforming work to be accomplished in you. But true change comes when your words become reality. An instant yes to God needs to be followed by *immediate action*. You push play. You take a concrete step and put obedience into motion. Not when it's convenient or when you find the time. . . . You take action *now*. There is a substantial difference between saying yes and doing something about it. As my friend Pastor Steven Furtick says, "The right time to do the right thing is right now." Immediate action is where the rubber meets the road and real change is effected.

To repeatedly say yes and not follow through is the equivalent of saying no.

I would love to tell you that that has always been my response to God, but it hasn't. There have been promptings I've overlooked, whispers I've edited or postponed responding to. Those instances have been costly and often led to pain and hurt that could have been avoided if I had said yes and followed with immediate action.

Fortunately, sitting in that church in Chicago was not one of those times. The moment that session was over at Willow Creek, I walked out of the auditorium and called my wife, Jacki. After that conversation, I called my boss, Ron, and set up a time to tell him what had happened so that he could help guide me into "the next" that God had for me.

An instant yes to God is only activated when it's ignited by immediate action.

"Just say a simple, 'Yes, I will,' or 'No, I won't'" (Matthew 5:37).

To repeatedly say yes and not follow through is the

equivalent of saying no. Not only is it disingenuous, but it short-circuits your Transformation Adventure.

You don't just say you're going to forgive someone—you text them now to arrange a meeting; you pick up the phone and call. You have the conversation.

You don't just say you're going to write that check—you pull out your checkbook, pick up a pen, write it, and send it—now.

You don't just say you're going to get serious about growing spiritually—you show up at church; you grapple with the messages; you spend time in the Bible; you commit to a plan that connects you with real community.

Remember, *someday* is a cussword. You've only got one life—what are you waiting for?

NO NEGOTIATING

When you're armed with an *instant yes* and you've taken *immediate action*, there is one final key that unleashes transformation and freedom in your life: *no negotiating*. None. It's saying to God, "I don't need to understand the details. I don't need to make sense of how this plays out. I don't need to sit at some imaginary boardroom table negotiating with You, God. I leave the how to You." It's choosing to believe that if God is the One who called this, then it's best.

I may have seemed a little nonchalant in describing how I began the process of quitting my job at that conference in Chicago, but honestly, when I said yes to God, I knew it wasn't going to be simple. Jacki and I were about to have our first baby. I was already wrestling with the normal fears that first-time fathers have: What if I throw up on my baby when I change a poopy diaper? What if I'm playing with this baby and accidentally rip off an arm? Now I also had to deal with the reality that Jacki was about to quit her job in anticipation of the baby's arrival. We would be stepping out with no guarantee of an income and no backup plan. There were plenty of things that could have made me nervous and unsure about stepping into the unknown, but that didn't stop me. Jacki and I spent focused time praying through this decision together, but frankly, it was never about the details. While there had been times in our lives when the presence of real challenges seemed too daunting to move forward, we were determined this time to respond with audacious trust. We knew that if God calls you, He has you.

> If God calls you, He has you.

COURAGEOUS STEPS

When you take courageous steps along this path, you're not the first. You not only follow in the footsteps of those who've walked it before you, but you ultimately follow in Jesus' footsteps. He is our prime example. He responded to every whisper of the Father with instant obedience and concrete action, and He changed the world (see John 8:28). With Jesus as our example, we can follow the finger of God tracing the path of our Transformation Adventure that will lead us to real, immediate, and lasting change. The power of God will be released in your life through agreement in even the smallest action steps. You will find the bully of sin getting his tail kicked in your life and an emerging freedom that comes from the Spirit of God doing some long-awaited redemptive work.

I've watched scores of people walk this path in the nearly fifteen years since we started the church that God called us to launch that unforgettable day at Willow Creek. They have been real people with real challenges and real lives who decided they were going to make real war. They started saying yes and pushing play, as real action began to take place through their agreement with God. Their lives, our church, and our city began to look remarkably different.

> The power of God will be released in your life through agreement in even the smallest action steps.

Like them, you may find yourself looking different next week, and the week after, and the week after that. At some point, you will look back and realize that your "Maybe Someday" file has been permanently deleted as you push play and begin actually living the plans God has for you. You will emerge a different person—not because of this book, or even because you really meant to—but because if you're a follower of Christ, the same Spirit that raised Jesus from the dead lives in you and you are agreeing with Him!

So what about it? What are you going to do with all of this? It's not just about arriving at a destination; it's about the journey. And God's Transformation Adventure for your life is most definitely a journey. I compel you to begin the path comprised of real yeses and real actions. If you're willing to throw your hat in the ring and go for it—then let's push play now and come directly to God for His help. This needs to be an active conversation with Him every step of the way. So why don't we begin with a simple prayer I've prayed with thousands of people.

It's a prayer of agreement, a prayer giving God that crack in the door He's been longing for. . . . It's about the end of "someday" and the beginning of a life of pushing play *now*. If you've got it in you, I'd encourage you to stand to your feet (a posture of action) and extend your hands, palms up (a posture of agreement). I invite you to begin each chapter of this book by praying this Transformation Adventure prayer with an open and sincere heart, inviting God to do His resurrecting work in you. Ready? Let's pray this from the bottom of our hearts. . . .

A PRAYER OF TRANSFORMATION

God, thank You for inviting me into this Transformation Adventure. Today I choose to push play on the life You have for me. Speak to my heart, stir me out of complacency, and transform me into the wholehearted follower of Jesus You created me to be. I surrender the fears and hesitations that keep me from making real progress in my walk with You. Thank You for loving me and empowering me with Your Spirit. Transform me from the inside out. Today, I will take action on what You show me—without negotiating. I will agree with Your work in my life. You have my yes in advance. I'm not waiting for someday, God; I'm pushing play now. Amen!

GETTING TRACTION

⏪ REWIND

God provides the power; we provide the agreement.

⬇ DOWNLOAD

The Spirit of God, who raised Jesus from the dead, lives in you. And just as God raised Christ Jesus from the dead, he will give life to your mortal bodies by this same Spirit living within you. ROMANS 8:11

▶ PUSH PLAY

Determine what's holding you back from following God's prompting. Now respond to Him with an instant yes, immediate action, and no negotiating.

Chapter 3

LET THEM GO

HAVE YOU EVER SEEN people try to do something they were lousy at? I mean, waaaay out of their zone, something they had no business doing, but they were totally clueless? The kind of thing that makes you think, *Why didn't someone tell them?*

Yep—I'm thinking Round 1, *American Idol.*

Those poor people! They sing their lungs out, torturing us and blowing out our eardrums. And as they sing, two things are going through every viewer's mind:

1. Stop!!!
2. Why didn't someone tell them *they can't sing?*
   (*before* they were on national television?)

The judges ask the question that's on everyone's mind: "Who encouraged you to audition?" They start listing people close to them—Mom, Dad, friends, etc. It's then that you start to realize that either the folks they've surrounded themselves with are exceptionally under-talented, or they just didn't have the courage to do the loving thing and tell these people they probably shouldn't sing—not in the car, not even in the shower.

But nobody tells them.

Why? Because most people tell each other what they want to hear instead of lovingly giving someone what he *needs* to hear.

Now, I'm no *American Idol* judge so I can't comment on your singing. (You sound pretty good from here!) However, in this chapter, I *am* about to say some things that may be difficult to hear. Please stick with me—it may not be easy, but I promise it will save you a world of regret and hurt for years and years to come.

Ready? Let's start someplace familiar . . . the Bible.

ALL TANGLED UP

Therefore, since we are surrounded by such a great
cloud of witnesses, let us throw off everything that
hinders and the sin that so easily entangles, and let us
run with perseverance the race marked out for us.

HEBREWS 12:1, NIV

There are three things that stand out in that verse for me. First, if you've ever felt alone—like no one understands the situation you're facing—the Bible says there is a great cloud of witnesses cheering you on. What's a "cloud of witnesses"? They are the people who have taken the Transformation Adventure, run the race, and finished the course. They are now with God in heaven watching your progress. They cheer for you because you're following Christ, just as they followed Christ. They can see with perfect clarity that He is the One worth following. When you grow weary, remember that they have been where you've been and are pulling for you!

Second, there is sin in our lives that we consistently choose. It entangles us and prevents us from running the race God has set for us. While the cloud of witnesses is cheering you on in Christ, the sin you've chosen is fighting against you, holding you back.

Third, in order to run the race, we need to throw off that sin that has wrapped itself around us. We need to reject it and be done with it.

Easier said than done.

A couple of summers ago, I was at a lake house with the Quest Community worship team, and after working on some songs for QCC's first worship album, we found ourselves up late—hanging out and laughing together. Around 3 a.m., just as most of them were headed off to bed, I suggested we take a boat ride. Seriously, how often do you get to go on a boat ride at that crazy hour? It was pitch-dark and slightly raining, but the offer was irresistible and we went for it!

The temperature of the water was perfect—about 88 degrees, even at night. We cruised our rented pontoon boat over to a secluded corner of the lake and jumped in, each carrying a life vest so we could just enjoy floating around in the warm water and talking. However, the last person in—a very inexperienced boatsperson (who shall remain nameless)—disembarked with exactly the kind of flourish we were all hoping to avoid, the one that shot the floating pontoon boat backward across the lake.

Now I will give Connie (oops!) credit—she did leave the boat with a mounted flashlight, which helped us see it from a distance. But it's really quite amazing how far a boat can drift when you pay little to no attention to it for over two hours.

At some point we realized that if we didn't want to swim home, someone was going to have to go and retrieve the abandoned boat floating all the way across the lake.

Nice to meet you. My name is Someone.

After a long swim with a friend of mine, I finally made it to within a few yards of the boat, which by now had floated near a shoreline. I had managed to close the gap to just a couple of feet when something underneath the water suddenly grabbed my legs!

It wasn't my friend.

I didn't know who or what it was, but I felt like I was an unwilling extra in an eighties' slasher movie. At the time, it seemed like a reasonable option in the dead of night in the middle of a deserted lake I'd never been to before.

I fought back and managed to free one leg. Then whatever was holding me somehow snaked itself around both of my legs. I was trapped, unable to move forward. For a moment

I debated screaming, but I collected myself. If I was going to die, it was going to be with at least some measure of dignity.

No one knew the danger I was in; my head was still above water—for the moment. Heart pounding, I reached for the boat rope dangling in the water, grabbed it, and tried to pull myself free. After a brief struggle, I finally made it; I was loose.

My mystery underwater pursuer? Not a deranged maniac. Not the remains of an ancient shipwreck. Not even something from *River Monsters*. Just some stray wires, lines, and a few tree branches reaching up from the bottom of the lake.

So why am I telling you this story? Those trees and wires didn't drown me. I was never close to losing my life or a leg. The simple reality was that I could tread water, bob in place, but I couldn't move forward. Despite the appearance of being okay, I was really stuck—all tangled up.

Here's the gift you may not want but might really need: You're not going to go very far on this Transformation Adventure until you get unstuck from the sin that has entangled you and is holding you back from running the race God has set for you.

Sometimes the sin that entangles us is obvious. We're aware of it, we've nursed it, we've protected it; it's become familiar to us. It's a ball and chain around your walk with God, and there's no need for you to manage it one more day. You can simply come before the One who never tires of forgiving, humble yourself, acknowledge your guilt, and let Him wash you clean today. Deal with what's obvious. It's far easier than dealing with some sins that are less apparent.

Other times, our noses tell us that something smells fishy, but we're just not sure exactly what it is. Just like the underwater branches and wires, sometimes there's something lurking below the surface, and we don't necessarily know what's got us.

Perhaps the sin that entangles you wasn't even originally yours.

TOXIC

We've all been hurt, and sometimes that hurt goes deep. The damage is costly; we lose sleep, joy, the ability to trust, an eagerness to laugh, and even intimacy with the people who love us most. We tend to think that's just life, and hurt happens. *It shouldn't have gone that way, but it did so I'd better just get over it.* However, what we often overlook is this: mishandled hurt robs us of God's transforming work in our lives. When we leave hurt unchecked, it just simmers like a hot poison inside, corroding our hearts and stopping the flow of God's power to transform our lives. It leaves us stuck and tangled up. You might be able to keep your head above water and look like you're inching in the right direction, but you're not running the race that's been set out for you by God if you don't deal with what's lurking under the surface.

Phrased another way, you're not going to get very far in your transformation journey until you deal with the sin of unforgiveness in your life.

I know what you're thinking:

Hold up. Did you just call unforgiveness a sin?
Rape is a sin. Abuse is a sin. Stealing, cheating, lying are sins.
You're going to call unforgiveness sin? Be careful.

I've found that when most people take that stance, they are usually on the verge of rationalizing why it's okay to hold on to resentment against another person.

But let me stop you; I'm not trying to be insensitive. Things happened to you that never should have happened and that can't be undone.

> Mishandled hurt robs us of God's transforming work in our lives.

I'm so sorry for what you endured, friend. I truly am.

But unforgiveness isn't the answer. It never rights the wrongs you've experienced, and if you've nursed unforgiveness and self-pity, then something has begun to grow inside of you. It has likely become toxic, and you can't afford to let it infect your life one more day. You've got to deal with the sin.

Why is it a sin again? The entire New Testament is filled with verses that basically say, "Forgive, forgive, forgive." Forgive your enemy, do good to those who harm you, love them, serve them, turn your other cheek to them. Over and over Jesus' message was one of forgiveness. He preached it, practiced it, and finally gave up His life to embody it on the cross.

Anytime you're going the opposite direction of the Cross of Christ, it's sin. Anytime you're disobeying God, it's sin.

Have you ever wondered why you can't seem to get traction or build lasting momentum in your spiritual life? Have you ever just said, "I don't know what the deal is—I get on the transformation path, I start out with good intentions, but somehow I get tripped up"? While there is a handful of primary reasons that we get tripped up, one that is commonly overlooked is the issue of unforgiveness—people's actions that we haven't let go of, and as a result, they haven't let go of us. Is it possible that God is highlighting for you the cancer of unforgiveness because it is wreaking havoc in your inner world, damaging components of your heart, mind, and soul? And as a result, your life is shrinking. Your ability to trust is evaporating; your personality is shifting. Avoidance has become a normal practice, and you're skimming through relationships, no longer risking your heart on anyone. You've become somebody who doesn't have the capacity to say an instant yes to God and take immediate action because you've got too many walls built with the bricks of unforgiveness.

> Anytime you're going the opposite direction of the Cross of Christ, it's sin.

What life are you waiting for to deal with it? You may be wondering why I am focusing on this topic at such an early point in our Transformation Adventure. In my decades of pastoring, I've seen the same thing time and time again: people start strong on their journey with great intentions, only to find themselves stuck—stuck in weeds of unforgiveness, unable to make significant progress until they honestly deal with this pivotal topic. I'm going to tell you this *American Idol* style: You can't manage unforgiveness! It's not your friend. You can't treat it like it's a roommate. Don't even try. If you do, you'll die just a little bit more each day.

WHAT'S YOUR FOCUS?

I was sitting on the bleachers when it happened.

My son's football team was supposed to be crushing the opponent, but the referees weren't up to speed on this reality. Yellow flag after yellow flag had been thrown. Two straight touchdowns had been recalled. What began as an innocent game started to feel like a malicious vendetta against a team of eight-year-olds. The tension was mounting.

With only a few moments to go in the game, the break we had been looking for finally came—and I was the only one who saw it! The coach for the opposing team was standing on the field with his team, a clear violation of NFL regulations! I jumped to my feet, cleared my throat, and was about to let these prison-guards-turned-referees have it, when my eyes spotted something that stopped me in my tracks: my son's coach was *also* standing on the field with his players. Over multiple seasons with my sons in this league, I had totally overlooked (or had chosen to ignore) that in this age group, the football coach is *always* on the field with his team. My perception that the opposite team was cheating was fueled by my indignation at the treatment my son's team was receiving. Fortunately, sanity prevailed, and I humbly—and silently— took my seat.

What you focus on matters.

When we find ourselves hurt, what do we tend to focus on? Ourselves. My hurt, my pain, my rights, my feelings. All too quickly we find ourselves fully absorbed with the brokenness of what happened when we were deserted, rejected, falsely accused, bullied, abused, or overlooked. We generally focus on "me and mine," and when self is what we're focusing on, most other things tend to get distorted and ignored.

We also tend to focus on *them*—the ones who hurt us.

So where is your focus? Who are your offenders? Who are the two or three people who immediately come to mind? If you have to brainstorm, you're on the wrong track. Who is it that hurt you? Get a picture of them in your mind, because if you're going to deal with this, then you must deal with them! To truly let them go, you need to identify specifically who you're talking about and what they did. The boss who was unfair, the mother who should have loved you, the father who left, the husband who betrayed you, the friend who offended you. Get them in your mind.

An apology will not bring healing. Only the Cross of Jesus Christ is the antidote to the unforgiveness in your heart.

Notice, I did not say get them in your mind so you can pray for them to come say they're sorry. This is not about an apology. The majority of the time those who hurt you will never apologize. Most of the time they won't even agree that they did anything to hurt you. They see it differently than you do.

And I have bad news for you—an apology will not bring healing.

Only the Cross of Jesus Christ is the antidote to the unforgiveness in your heart. As the apostle Paul writes,

Through him God reconciled everything to himself.
He made peace with everything in heaven and on
earth by means of Christ's blood on the cross.
COLOSSIANS 1:20

Once you've experienced God's forgiveness (vertically),
you'll then have the power to offer forgiveness (horizontally).
When you start to forgive, you'll start to grow. You'll start
to be transformed by the power of God, and you'll start to
thrive. You'll be on the path that's been set out for you, and
you'll find yourself running God's race for your life.

Which is why the writer of Hebrews continues with an
unforgettable key to the Transformation Adventure God has
called us to:

Let us fix our eyes on Jesus, the author and perfecter
of our faith.   HEBREWS 12:2, NIV

Focus on Jesus.

You want to know how to run this race all the way to the
finish and join the cloud of witnesses? Focus on Jesus as He
washes the feet of those who will soon abandon Him. Would
you like to cut the weight that's been breaking your back and
slowing you down? Look at Jesus asking His Father to forgive
those who are nailing Him to the cruel cross. Would you like
to finally experience freedom and live an unencumbered, bless-
able life? Observe how Jesus handles being mistreated by the
very people He was laying His life down to rescue and redeem.

What we consume, consumes us. What you focus on shapes you. What you fix your gaze on will ultimately begin to shape your life.

> What we consume, consumes us. What you focus on shapes you.

Remember what your mom used to tell you? "Garbage in, garbage out!" It's like that, only in reverse. When Jesus lives in you and you focus on Him, His character begins to flow out of you. Even in the face of being treated in ways we should never be treated, when our eyes are fixed on Jesus, we learn to give love, mercy, forgiveness, and grace as freely as He gives them to us.

A NEW MATH

It's not the easiest pill to swallow. In fact, even the people closest to Jesus had a hard time getting this one straight. In Matthew 18, the apostle Peter approached Jesus concerning this very topic, looking for some parameters on the concept of forgiveness.

> Then Peter came to him and asked, "Lord, how often should I forgive someone who sins against me? Seven times?" MATTHEW 18:21

I don't suspect that Peter really forgot how many times you're supposed to forgive someone. Peter knew, according to Jewish law, that he was supposed to forgive someone three times. I think Peter is trying to look impressive, so he blows a little smoke. He's trying to look magnanimous, so he doubles it and adds some for good measure. But in the end Peter doesn't get the gold star he's looking for:

> "No, not seven times," Jesus replied, "but seventy times seven!" MATTHEW 18:22

You can imagine Peter doing quick math in his head. *We should forgive 490 times? Are you serious? Who will keep track? What's the system? Who will be the judge?* But Jesus wasn't speaking as a twenty-first century mathematician, revealing the algorithm of forgiveness; He was explaining the heart of our great God. God forgives people who don't deserve it; who don't even want it or know that they need it. Jesus' point is to illustrate that God gives what we don't deserve—God gives grace. And He pours His forgiveness into each of us, that we might spill it out into others. As my colleague Perry Noble says, "Forgiven people forgive people."

Since this revolutionary principle wasn't quite sinking in for Peter, Jesus went on to tell a story to drive His point home.

> Forgiven people forgive people.

> Therefore, the Kingdom of Heaven can be compared to a king who decided to bring his accounts up to date with servants who had borrowed money from him. In the process, one of his debtors was brought in who owed him millions of dollars. He couldn't pay, so his master ordered that he be sold—along with his

wife, his children, and everything he owned—to pay
the debt.

But the man fell down before his master and
begged him, "Please, be patient with me, and I will
pay it all." Then his master was filled with pity for
him, and he released him and forgave his debt.

But when the man left the king, he went to a
fellow servant who owed him a few thousand dollars.
He grabbed him by the throat and demanded instant
payment.

His fellow servant fell down before him and
begged for a little more time. "Be patient with
me, and I will pay it," he pleaded. But his creditor
wouldn't wait. He had the man arrested and put in
prison until the debt could be paid in full.

When some of the other servants saw this, they
were very upset. They went to the king and told
him everything that had happened. Then the king
called in the man he had forgiven and said, "You evil
servant! I forgave you that tremendous debt because
you pleaded with me. Shouldn't you have mercy on
your fellow servant, just as I had mercy on you?"

MATTHEW 18:23-33

I'll never forget when I first heard Bill Hybels preach on
this story with precision and power during a weekend service
at Willow Creek Community Church. This Scripture passage
marked me then and has continued to shape me since, and

offers us key lessons that are essential if we hope to make war on unforgiveness.

GOD'S ECONOMY

Verse 24 says, "In the process, one of his debtors was brought in who owed him millions of dollars." "Millions of dollars" is a rough translation of what the text says. The amount that's actually stated is "ten thousand talents," which in the first century equated to about five thousand lifetimes' worth of earnings. In other words, Jesus is saying it's an impossible debt that the servant will never be able to repay. This man is in serious trouble.

Forgiveness Is Always Expensive

Notice, though, when the king releases the man's debt, it doesn't just vanish. When a debt is forgiven, it doesn't just disappear, right? The reality is that someone always has to pay; someone has to absorb the loss. In this case, it's the king. He pays this ridiculous price. Why? Because forgiveness is always expensive!

In fact, sin will always take you further than you wanted to go and cost you more than you ever wanted to pay. Paul's words in Romans 6:23 capture that tragic picture perfectly: "For the wages of sin is death . . ."

Just ask Lorrie, whose flirting turned into a full-blown affair that nearly destroyed her family.

> Sin will always take you further than you wanted to go and cost you more than you ever wanted to pay.

Or Jim, whose internal evaluations grew into a critical spirit that nearly ended his ministry.

Katie's judgmentalism became an armor of anger, pride, and emotional isolation.

Todd's foray into pornography ambushed his plans for youth ministry.

Dana's materialism turned into crippling debt that still holds her hostage.

The truth is that we've all built such a steep sin-debt before God that we will never be able to pay our entire bill. Never! You will never atone for your own sins; therefore you'll never be able to make yourself right with God. And this is the even more astonishing truth—Jesus voluntarily assumed responsibility for your sin-debt. When you put your trust in Him, He settles your account in full, as the five people I mentioned above are experiencing firsthand. Each of them is now living in the grace, healing, and redemption that only God can give. You will never save up the resources to pay for what only Jesus can.

Some of us have grown up in the church and have "known" these truths for a long time, but nonetheless we're striving to cover our own tab. If you're trying to earn God's forgiveness through your performance, it's a pointless endeavor. You are trying to pay a bill that's already been settled. Others of you are just now understanding this great truth and have yet to trust Christ to cover your deficit. Currently you are responsible for your debt, but be encouraged—Jesus' offer is open to you even today.

In light of the high and painful price Christ paid to offer us forgiveness, doesn't it stand to reason that it will come at quite a painful price to us to forgive others? It's not cheap; it's extremely expensive. It costs you your rights. You freely offer up your right to be understood, your right to make them pay, your right to hold them responsible, and your right to an apology. When you forgive someone, you deliberately give up your plea for what's fair. In the same way that Christ doesn't give you what you deserve, you stop wishing that they'll get what they deserve. You give them grace, just as He gives you grace.

You let them go and you clear the record in your heart that contains the charges against them. It's expensive and it's costly and it's painful. But you're following after the One who went first. The One who showed us how.

Forgiveness Is Never Deserved

> But the man fell down before his master and begged him, "Please, be patient with me, and I will pay it all." Then his master was filled with pity for him, and he released him and forgave his debt.
>
> MATTHEW 18:26–27

This servant was not a good guy. To run up a 10,000-talent tab, this guy was living beyond his means for his entire adult life. Even in Vegas you'd have to work at it to rack up a bill that high. He had been out of control, and now his day of reckoning was here. In the first century, his path of repayment was well understood by all of Jesus' listeners: First, you were sold into slavery, then your wife was sold into slavery, then your children were sold into slavery. If that wasn't enough, their children and their children's children were part of the deal as well. Your family was destroyed and would go on to live as slaves to pay the debt that would never be satisfied. Simply put, this guy's life was ruined.

And then the twist comes. As they are dragging him away, he is pleading, and the king looks at him and feels compassion. He reaches down, takes the guy by the arm, and says, "On your feet. You're not going to be sold as a slave. Your wife and children will not be slaves. You will keep your home and possessions. The debt you owe? Consider it satisfied! The grace period has been extended indefinitely. You're a debt-free man—walk away."

The Cross of Christ wasn't a logical response; it was the response of grace.

Do you know who this man is? He is *us*! You and I are the man in Jesus' parable. Moreover, that is precisely our standing before a holy God. We've sinned in so many different ways, sometimes even intentionally, and it's always against the One who has no sin, against our great, holy God. We deserve no forgiveness; we stand before Him with no argument to be made, entirely unworthy of forgiveness. So what case do we have? The only case you'll ever have—Jesus Christ!

When we were utterly helpless, Christ came at just the right time and died for us sinners. ROMANS 5:6

The Cross of Christ wasn't a logical response; it was the response of grace. The forgiveness offered isn't a gift deserved or earned; it is a gift of mercy and love.

. Truth be told, much of the hurt you've suffered should never have happened and those responsible shouldn't have done what they did. But if you continue to demand payment from them, you are setting yourself up for a graceless, cynical, suspicious, and shrinking life. Your Transformation Adventure will be substantially slowed as you drag this unnecessary weight behind you. In large part, you'll struggle to push play and follow God in freedom until you deal with this. Two fundamentals to keep on the forefront of your mind: forgiveness is never deserved, and Jesus alone is your way out.

Forgiveness Isn't an Event, It's a Lifestyle

"Shouldn't you have mercy on your fellow servant,
just as I had mercy on you?" MATTHEW 18:33

This isn't a nice, sweet question from the king. This was a rhetorical question meaning, "You should have shown mercy! Son, I gave you grace, and it's in your best interest to give grace to others. I forgave you, and you ought to be a forgiver of others! I released your huge debt; you ought to have done the same for their tiny bill! What were you thinking?" This chastisement from the king seems like the appropriate response in light of this servant's heartless encounter with a fellow servant; after all, in verse 28 this servant grabs a guy by the throat, demanding payment for an unpaid debt. He did not understand the forgiveness just given to him. He receives grace and treats it as though it is something he's entitled to. In return, he doesn't even blink as he ruthlessly demands from someone else.

What about you? Do you view the forgiveness God offers you as something remarkable or as something common? Are you undone by it as an unspeakable gift of love, or, truth be told, do you feel somehow entitled to it like a spoiled child at Christmastime throwing boxes and bows, continually looking for what's next?

Consider this: when Christ died in your place, He offered forgiveness for all your sins, even the hidden, secret ones. Even for those, there is lavish exoneration. Not just for regrettable deeds, but thoughts also; accidental trespasses and premeditated acts of rebellion. God, in His rich love, offers to erase them all as He covers them in the blood of His one and only Son, whom He gave up for this purpose.

In the face of all God has done to forgive you, doesn't it make sense that you would forgive them—whoever "they" are to you? Doesn't it make sense that you would let them go? No matter what they've done to you, you don't want to be the man in Jesus' story who *receives* in great abundance and *withholds* in small pittances, right? "Forgiven people forgive people."

> God poured His forgiveness *into* us so it would spill *out of* us.

Then why do we live in verse 28 so much of the time? Why do we demand what's ours? God poured His forgiveness *into* us so it would spill *out of* us. When Jesus looked at Peter and said, "Forgive, forgive, forgive 490 times," it wasn't a rule! That's not forgiveness. Forgiveness is a response of the heart, mind, and will all working together. It's never true forgiveness if it's simply a matter of dutiful obedience. That's reminiscent of my fifteen-year-old, who, with arms crossed and a scowl on his face, begrudgingly announces to his ten-year-old brother, "Okay then, I forgive you."

> You cancel their record, and by doing so, *you* are liberated.

Forgiveness is a heart condition where you let someone off the hook for good.

Try reading that last sentence again, out loud and slowly this time. When Jesus tells us to become forgiving people, He's saying, "I've poured this into you, and in the same way I give you grace, extend it. Let them go . . . clear their record. Let them off the hook. Give up your rights to be understood, to be pitied, and to make them pay." It doesn't justify what they did. It just stops your heart from growing toxic and suffering the torture all over again.

Surprisingly, as you free them from your anger and wrath, you begin to experience a divine freedom. You cancel their record, and by doing so, *you* are liberated. It allows you the freedom to grow in Christ and be transformed.

LETTING THEM GO

In light of our standing before God and the urgency of our need to live as forgiven people who forgive people, I offer you these three traction steps—a "how-to" for releasing people and actually letting them go. It doesn't change what they did to you or the fact that their behavior may have profoundly impacted your life. It simply means you are following in Jesus' footsteps, forgiving their debt against you, and as a result, you escape the entanglement of unforgiveness. This is how you move forward:

1. *Reflect on the grace God has given to you.* Spend fifteen minutes and think through the ways He's shown you grace. Name some actual sins in your past that He has forgiven. Get before the cross and say, "You gave me grace when I said that, when I went through that season, when I blew You off there, when I said I loved You and didn't live like it, when I didn't respect my husband or love my wife." Name it specifically. As Jesus teaches in Luke 7, he who has been forgiven much, loves much. So sometimes you may need to dig deep so that you can really understand how much He's forgiven you.

   (If you haven't placed your trust in Christ and experienced His forgiveness, I suggest you jump ahead and read chapter ten, where I'll help you do exactly that. It may be one of the most important chapters you'll ever read.)

2. *Name your offenders.* Name the specific ways they hurt you. Don't demonize them; try to get rid of the

exaggeration. Name them and get clear on how they hurt you. It could be as simple as "Here's what they said, here's what they did, and here's who it was." Let Jesus meet you in your pain; let Him have access to the specific places where you've built up walls and to the precise people you've held captive.

3. *Release them to God.* Let them go. Forgive them. Give the offense to Jesus, the ultimate Judge who will one day make all things right. In the shadow of the cross, clear the record and let them go.

You may be thinking, "How can I just let them go? Do you know what they did to me?" And the answer is "No, I don't." But if you haven't let them go, I have a hunch I know what it's *still* doing to you.

I know you're stuck in the weeds and barely keeping your head above water, wishing that you could be transformed by God, hoping that someday you will become a more loving, trusting, gracious, tenderhearted person. Some of us have pushed this down so deep and ignored it for so long that it's become normal to do life entrenched in our resentment. We have a hard time being intimately connected to anyone in our lives. Anger comes out of nowhere. We can't list very many ways we've grown and been transformed by the power of God. We're still carrying unforgiveness, and it's siphoning away our hearts, crimping the conduit of the power of God that is meant to run freely into our lives.

Your marriage will never be whole until forgiveness is given and received. Your kids will never know what it means to love sacrificially and what it means to be a follower of Christ until this is dealt with in your life. You'll never restore the honor in your relationships with your parents, your siblings, or that friend until you let them go.

When we stand before a bloodstained cross, it doesn't make a lot of sense that He would forgive us completely of all our guilty stains, yet we would withhold forgiveness from others. I don't know who it was or what they did, but I know you don't need to rehash it one more time.

You can let them go! And when you do, you'll experience freedom that you never imagined possible. Need proof? Read some inescapable evidence in this letter my executive pastor, Sharon, and I recently received from our friend Leslie:

Dear Pastor Pete and Sharon,

It was three years ago today that Jon admitted his affair and decided to leave. I thought August 6 would be a day that I hated for the rest of my life. Thank you for making a place where he could come. Pastor Pete, you had just started the "God Can" series, and he heard about how God can rebuild the rubble of our lives. About a month later, when it all went public, God gave Jon a clear picture of what he had done, and the truth he had heard became reality. Thank you for having a recovery ministry like The Mat, where he could go and do the real work

*freedom requires. I had already filed for a divorce when
I started attending, but I was looking for hope. I knew
I wanted to forgive Jon, but I didn't know where to begin.
As I experienced the love and grace and truth of that
community, the walls of self-protection and control began
to crumble.*

*One week at my small group, I made a list of all of the
material things, relationships, and dreams I had lost as
a result of Jon's choices. After making an exhaustive list,
Jesus offered me a choice. I could make Jon pay me back
for the pieces of my heart and my life that he had broken,
or I could choose to cancel the debt he owed me. It was
excruciating, but I made my choice and wrote "Paid In
Full" across the pages of my journal.*

*What God did to rebuild our lives since that decision
has been nothing short of remarkable. His freedom and
healing have flooded my heart and our marriage. In
November of 2010, I filed a motion to stop the divorce.
A month later we found out I was pregnant . . . with
twins. The risky step to forgive and trust Jon again
unleashed the potential for our marriage and our children's
future. For all the death and destruction that the enemy
plotted for our family, Jesus was writing another story: one
of life, and hope, and grace.*

*And while we both celebrated God's remarkable
redemption, we thought we were surely disqualified from
having any real impact. But this culture of grace and
redemption showed us otherwise. You gave us the chance*

to share what He had done in the middle of our mess. That He could make the redemption of our family as public as its destruction was. And as we've shared God's amazing redemption of our marriage and family, He's used our story to offer hope—to friends, seekers, even pastors and their wives who have found hope and healing . . . through us!

Thank you for making a place for us to come . . . for believing that God uses everything for good and taking a risk on us. Thank you for seeing the calling on my husband's life and letting him lead worship. I really think he was born for this.

And this day, that I thought I would hate for the rest of my life, is now a day that I am thankful for. Jon and I are both living out our callings for the good of the Bride these days, and I am so, so grateful.

I cannot believe this is my life.

Love,
Leslie

He supplies the power; we supply the agreement. Perhaps your Transformation Adventure will finally take off the moment you have a courageous and transparent conversation with God. If you're ready to stop wishing and waiting for "time to heal all wounds," this active prayer may be a great way to start:

God, thank You for forgiving me time and time again. Thank You for the extravagant gift of grace in the death of Your Son for my sins. Right now, I ask for Your forgiveness for how I've clutched the hurts in my life and embraced unforgiveness, even when I didn't know it. Please forgive me for my sin. I need Your help.

Father, I come humbly before the cross of Christ, ready to release to You those who hurt me. Lord, You know (insert their names) hurt me when they (name what they did), and it made me feel (describe how it made you feel). But in light of the grace given me, I choose to give them grace. I forgive them. I choose to let them off the hook. By Your power I clear their record against me. I surrender them to You and leave them at the cross, along with all the offenses and pain.

Jesus, I ask for Your healing grace to pour over me; set me free from all that has entangled me. Cover me with Your love and fill me anew with Your Spirit, and I pray that You would do the same for (the people you just forgave). Thank You for loving me and for Your gift and example of forgiveness on the cross. I pray this from the bottom of my heart in Jesus' name. Amen.

GETTING TRACTION

⏪ REWIND

Forgiveness is never deserved, and Jesus alone is your way out.

⬇ DOWNLOAD

"I forgave you that tremendous debt because you pleaded with me. Shouldn't you have mercy on your fellow servant, just as I had mercy on you?"
MATTHEW 18:32–33

▶ PUSH PLAY

Take the concrete steps to let them go:
1. Reflect on the grace God has given to you.
2. Name your offenders.
3. Release them to God.

Chapter 4

WITHOUT NETS

ALLOW ME TO INTRODUCE you to Charles Blondin.

In 1859, Chuck was all the rage. As one of the best tight-rope walkers on planet Earth, Blondin had made quite a name for himself. However, his crowning achievement was his seemingly effortless stroll across a tightrope suspended above the raging water of Niagara Falls. Hundreds had gathered to watch this extraordinary feat, and then went nuts as Chuck skipped across the millions of gallons of water cascading over the 167-foot drop.

But Blondin wasn't finished.

After making it across once, he came *back* across. And then went back across the tightrope again, this time on a bicycle. Blondin would proceed to cross the falls again and again without safety nets, taking it up a notch every time: blindfolded, on stilts, balancing on a chair with just one of its legs on the rope—all with such ease. The frenzy grew to the point where Blondin took a small stove out on his back and then cooked and ate an omelet while balancing on the tightrope! The crowds went wild. It seemed like there was nothing this man couldn't do.

So when he pulled a wheelbarrow out and raced it across the falls a couple of times, people played along, wondering what new jaw-dropping feat Blondin had up his sleeve. He shouted out to the crowd, "Do you think I can carry someone across the falls in this wheelbarrow?" Unfazed, the crowd shouted in reply, "Yes! Nothing can stop you—you can do this!" With a smile, Blondin shouted back, "Then who will volunteer and be my passenger in this wheelbarrow? Raise your hand!"

(Cue the crickets.)

Not a sound.

No one moved.

No one responded.

It was one thing to believe that Blondin could do it. It was altogether different to get in the wheelbarrow and actually trust your life to his skill.

We often deal with the same thing in our relationship with God. It's one thing to believe that God can do great things. It's another to get in His "wheelbarrow" and let Him attempt the impossible in your life!

JUST WATCH

It's all too easy to become a watcher. Someone who shouts encouragements from the sidelines, believing that God is capable of astonishing feats; even cheering on others who entrust themselves to God and allow Him to accomplish remarkable things through them. Watchers are near the action, but they never get too close to the tightrope.

Can I suggest to you that you were not made to be a watcher, an observer? You're not being who God designed you to be when you're sitting on the sidelines watching others participate in the breathtaking feats God is accomplishing.

I believe that you and I are designed to push play, to get in the wheelbarrow and experience the thrill of partnering with God in *this* life, not just the next. You were made by Him to join Him in accomplishing impossible exploits in His name. It's the adrenaline rush of knowing that if God drops you, you'll die, but even then, it's death in the hands of a loving God versus a slow fade on the sidelines of old age, comfortable with unworn shoes and soft hands.

Friend, the Son of God did not die on the cross to create a church full of watchers.

While His death on the cross accomplished the miraculous—forgiving your sins, rescuing you from hell, proving His love for you, and gaining your eternity in heaven—it also did more than that. He died to prove that you can trust Him, no matter what wheelbarrow He is calling you to get into. Jesus has a pretty remarkable track record; He has never dropped *anyone*.

So what life are you waiting for?

Here's the simply reality: *God will never be remarkable to you until you allow Him to do the remarkable* through *you.*

> God will never be remarkable to you until you allow Him to do the remarkable *through* you.

When God does His remarkable work through us, we begin to discover a whole new gear of awe and worship. This is just common sense. Take bungee jumping and cliff diving, for instance. It's one thing to watch with your mouth open and your feet safely on the ground, but once you experience them for yourself, you realize that you didn't comprehend even a fraction of the sheer exhilaration that comes from taking the leap. Now, multiply that feeling by a thousand or so, and you're starting to understand what it's like to be in the Transformation Adventure with God.

LET'S GO FISHING

You never know where an adventure is going to begin. Sometimes it's over Niagara Falls; sometimes adventures begin in a fishing boat.

In Luke 5 we catch an unforgettable moment: the first meeting of Jesus and Peter, one of His future apostles. In an interesting twist of events, it begins with history's first recorded boat-jacking! Jesus essentially hijacked Peter's commercial fishing boat to serve as His pulpit. Floating along the shoreline, Jesus taught to a crowded beach full of people eager to hear the Word of God. The Bible doesn't tell us what Peter (known at the time by his given name, Simon) thought of that sermon or how he felt about having Jesus hijack his boat. We get the impression that he's cleaning his nets, going about his business . . . watching.

I like to think that Simon was intrigued, and perhaps a bit impressed, by this rabbi from Nazareth who had the chutzpah to commandeer a grizzled fisherman's boat after a long night of fishing.

In fact, while writing this chapter, I went on a deep-sea fishing excursion with a few friends and my three favorite young men on the planet—Corey, Carson, and my godson, Renner. Leading us on the 52-foot Gulf Ranger was Captain David and his first mate, Michael. We had a great time, and we caught nearly a dozen good-size Red Snapper and King Mackerel. Throughout the trip, I was amazed at the captain's wealth of knowledge. He knew where to go, when to fish, and when to move.

Midway through our expedition, Corey got a strong tug on his line. He had clearly hooked something big and began to feverishly reel in his catch. After several minutes of fighting the choppy water, he finally triumphed and hauled our would-be lunch onto the boat. But as Corey and the rest of the gang began to cheer, our celebration was cut short when Michael abruptly grabbed this unusual fish in disgust. "This is not a good fish to catch. It's a leech fish, a remora, that scavenges the ocean. Throw it back. It's a nuisance, and we don't fish them." What began as excitement quickly turned into disappointment as we were scolded. These two pros knew their stuff and weren't taking input from anyone . . . not even paying customers. They were in charge of their fishing boat.

I can assure you, that day on the Sea of Galilee, Peter was in charge of his boat too. And while the Bible doesn't tell us what he was thinking in those first moments meeting Jesus on the Sea of Galilee, it does tell us what happened as Jesus' sermon in the boat wrapped up:

> When he had finished speaking, he said to Simon [Peter], "Now go out where it is deeper, and let down your nets to catch some fish."
>
> "Master," Simon replied, "we worked hard all last night and didn't catch a thing. But if you say so, I'll let the nets down again." LUKE 5:4-5

Isn't it crazy?

He's standing right in front of the Son of God—the Savior of the world—and Peter argues. He's tired of fishing; he knows it's pointless and he'll look like an idiot if he goes fishing at the wrong time of day. He just wants to go home and go to bed! He had just finished working third shift and was cleaning his nets. You can almost hear Peter: "Rabbi, loved the sermon, but this is a bad time to fish. We're exhausted. No offense, I really do appreciate the offer . . . "

Have you ever tried to procure the opportunity to spend time with someone influential, some highly sought after individual? I have. You make your best case and then you wait. You wait for the call, text, or e-mail, usually from an assistant, praying that the word you receive is yes—that they can spare a few minutes for a brief encounter or even a short lunch. If you're fortunate enough to get approval, then while you're still celebrating, you typically receive a list of terms and particulars that must be satisfied and fully agreed upon for your short visit to happen. It's intense, complicated, and anything but simple.

But in their first meeting, *Peter* is the one who receives the unanticipated invitation from the VIP! It's as if Jesus was tired after speaking and turned to Peter to request a simple boat ride across the Galilee. In the midst of this astonishing opportunity Peter basically says, "I'd rather not."

He tries to decline the offer by talking Jesus out of spending the day together. But he doesn't stop there; he begins to "educate" Jesus with his wisdom.

"With all due respect, Jesus, You're a teacher, not a fisherman. That's what I am. And this whole 'head-to-deeper-water' thing? It's a bad idea. You don't really understand all this, Lord."

Have you ever felt like that? Like Jesus may well understand the spiritual stuff—church, Communion, the Bible—but you wonder if He really understands *your* life?

He doesn't know how to be a mom or dad, right? Jesus can't relate to being a spouse in a tough marriage. He doesn't understand what it's like to be a recovering addict or to be diagnosed with cancer.

No matter what offer is on the table, we essentially respond with, "I appreciate Your heart and all, Jesus, but I don't think You can relate to my struggles, my family, my life. Thanks but no thanks."

Peter made it clear to Jesus: "I'm the fisherman, Rabbi. Why don't You just go home? You gave a great talk, everyone liked it, You drew really big crowds for Galilee. You've got the whole speaking thing down. Why do You want to wreck Your day by going fishing at noon?"

Jesus wasn't deterred. "Come on, Peter, let's go."

THE GRANDER VISION

Do you know how much Jesus really cared about fishing? Not very much.

Had Peter been a farmer, He would have said, "Let's go work the land." Had Peter been a construction worker, Jesus would have said, "Let's go frame some walls." (And with Jesus' carpentry training, He could have seriously schooled Peter in home improvement.)

But that day, His call was, "Hey, Peter, let's go fish."

Do you know what I believe? I believe that as Jesus looked at the man called Simon, He saw an entirely different life awaiting this fisherman from Capernaum—one that Peter hadn't even begun to dream of.

Jesus had far more in mind that day than a picturesque boat ride across the lake. He had beheld a grander vision.

He saw the one who would be known throughout the world down through the ages as "Peter the Rock."

He saw the day when only a few miles from this very spot,

with eyes wide and mouth agape, Peter would help pass out five loaves of bread and two fish, feed more than five thousand people, and collect twelve baskets of leftovers.

He beheld the night when eleven frightened disciples would watch in shock and awe as Peter stepped over the edge of this very same boat onto stormy seas and, with eyes fixed on Jesus, actually walked on water.

As He stepped into the boat that day, Jesus saw the moment when Peter would deny that he even knew Jesus—not once, but repeatedly.

He saw Peter running away at the split second when Jesus would need him most.

He saw the instant when, over breakfast on the beach, He would restore Peter with His unyielding love and relentless grace.

Jesus looked at Peter and saw the one who would step forward on the Day of Pentecost to launch and lead the very first church.

He saw the first three thousand people who would become Christians when Peter preached the very first sermon ever given in Jesus' name.

Jesus saw the day when Peter would be sent to jail for preaching about Him and yet refuse to stop.

And Jesus saw the final hours when Peter would die publicly, upside down on a cross as a martyr, worshipping the One who had first surrendered His life for him.

He saw a fisherman who would never again fish for perch, but would fish for people.

How's that for a grander vision for the life of a guy who, at this point, is just protesting and resisting—content to be an observer?

Do you ever find yourself there—stuck carrying out the routine, following in other people's footsteps? It takes an interruption by someone who sees a grander vision—in this case, Jesus—to stop us in our tracks and suggest an entirely alternate route, something bigger, something riskier, something that makes a difference. The apostle Paul nailed it when he said in Ephesians 1:11, "It's in Christ that we find out who we are and what we are living for" (*The Message*).

In other words, it's Jesus who leads us as we leave the predictable and make war on the mundane, the routine, and the safe. It's Jesus who gives us the courage to get in His wheelbarrow on the tightrope—without safety nets—and trust that He is actually leading us into the life we were created for, the life we've been waiting for. Our everyday life—taking care of business, doing what's expected—beckons us to play it safe, to stay small, to cheer on everyone else to do great things while we go about business as usual.

I can't even imagine what God has in store for you. You might be the next Billy Graham, Beth Moore, Lecrae, Tim Tebow, Condoleezza Rice, or Bill Hybels, but it's going to take an encounter with Jesus that snaps you out of your normal cadence and into a place that takes real faith, real risk, and real trust.

We need the lights to come on and fresh eyes to see that if we just keep the same heading we have now, we're going to live small, self-centered lives. Take it from Jesus as He struggles to get Peter out of that place and leave his nets behind: safe, self-consumed lives never change the world.

It takes a vision from Christ, ignited in the hearts and minds of average, ordinary people just like you and me, to catapult us into living bigger, Kingdom-minded lives—lives that make a difference long after we're gone.

> Safe, self-consumed lives never change the world.

And it doesn't begin with making headlines like Charles Blondin, doing death-defying feats. It starts with small steps of trusting Christ. For Peter, it was going out into deeper water and later leaving his nets behind. For you, it may be having the courage to tell your classmate or neighbor about what Jesus is doing in your life; it may be saying no to overtime to invest in a vibrant ministry of your church; it may be trusting God with your resources and becoming an underwriter of His ministry in spiritually destitute places. It doesn't have to be spectacular from the beginning; sometimes small steps are scary enough. But you must start somewhere. What are you going to do with His invitation?

In our passage, Jesus is trying to help Peter see His grander vision. "Just let Me lead you out to deeper places. Trust Me, it's not about fish. I'm going to show you what you've never seen before, something you will never forget and never recover from."

Peter finally relents. "But if you say so, I'll let the nets down again" (Luke 5:5).

"If You really want to go, we'll push off. Your call, Master. If You say so, Jesus, we'll go."

And so they did.

DEEPER WATER

Want to know what happens when you're with Jesus in deeper water?

I vividly recall the early days of starting Quest Community Church. Initially, we encountered things that felt impossible. Convincing people of a great vision, working to serve an entire city, capturing a crowd, securing a location, raising the resources, building teams, defining ministries, pulling off great services, helping people find hope. It all felt enormous, even insurmountable at times. And to all those along the way who say, "If God called it, He'll build it. No big deal, just relax," I say, you've obviously never planted a church. Sure, God provides, but "No big deal, nothing to worry about, just relax"? Please!

In those early years of establishing a new church, you do whatever it takes to be softhearted and open-eared to Jesus. I recall a "deeper water invitation" He had me extend to a volunteer on my teaching team. Helen and her husband, John, along with their three children, had helped me pioneer the church. Helen was a published author, a professor at the local seminary, and a great teacher. She also had a secret. Helen was an alcoholic. She had been perfectly upfront with me and a few trusted people in her life, but that's as far as the circle of those who knew stretched. Helen was a mature follower of Christ and hadn't had a drink for years.

As we approached the conclusion of a groundbreaking fall series, the Lord laid it on my heart that it was time to crack the code of a new level of authenticity in our church. After years of being Helen's pastor and close friend, I had a hunch that sharing her story was the key to opening up a deeper transparency in our church and expanding her influence in our community. It would begin by sharing what had been up until now a secret. I'll never forget the look on her face when I told her the challenge Jesus had given me for her. "I think it's time to go public, Helen. I think it's time to tell your story from the main stage." She was wide-eyed but calm and simply asked, "Are you serious?" Helen had been unmistakably called out to deeper water.

What's the deeper water for you? God knows about your life and the water you find yourself in. He knows your daily routine, all the familiar "nets" in your life (and how tired you are of them!). Have you ever been commuting to work and thought to yourself, *There must be more than this?* Ever gone to bed at night, exhausted from a full day, thinking, *Am I really accomplishing anything that matters? What am I here for? What did God really put me on the planet for in the first place?*

Today may well be the day Jesus hijacks your boat. Are you ready to follow Peter's example and respond with a "If you say so, I will" attitude to what Jesus suggests? If you do that, you might just find yourself with more than you can handle—in the best of ways.

> And this time their nets were so full of fish they
> began to tear! A shout for help brought their partners
> in the other boat, and soon both boats were filled
> with fish and on the verge of sinking.   LUKE 5:6-7

The professional fishermen freaked out! They were unprepared for what Jesus could do in deeper water.

But the huge catch of fish was just the beginning for Peter.

> When Simon Peter realized what had happened, he
> fell to his knees before Jesus and said, "Oh, Lord,
> please leave me—I'm too much of a sinner to be
> around you."   LUKE 5:8

It wasn't just that Peter was awed by Jesus' mad fishing skills. He knew that whatever was going on wasn't normal. In fact, it wasn't completely human. This was a "God thing," and Peter realized that they weren't just in deep water; he was in way over his head. From early in life, Peter had been trained to recognize that God was holy (meaning "separate" or "other") and that people were not. When Peter recognized the holy, he simultaneously recognized who wasn't. His sense of unworthiness was enough to make him push Jesus away.

Seems like the right response to holiness, doesn't it?

The only problem with this approach? Jesus wasn't pushing Peter away.

Peter was the one creating distance. Our sin separates us from God, but Jesus was there in the flesh, revealing the heart of God and declaring His intention to initiate a relationship with flawed, unholy people.

The evening when Helen and I spoke about going public with her secret was an important moment in her life as well as the life of our church. You see, she had to grapple with the obvious questions: What if I tell the church and people reject or mistrust me? What if they think I'm unfit to teach God's Word? What if my family is embarrassed, hurt, or wounded? Will I still be able to teach, lead, and serve in this church I love so much?

In addition, there were other questions that needed to be considered: Could our two-year-old fledgling church handle this potential scandal? Would people leave? After all, "Pastor Pete knew this about Helen when he asked her to be a part of the teaching team."

All this was summed up in Helen's question, "Are you serious?" And my answer was emphatic: "Absolutely!" If we were going to be a church that showed an accurate picture of who Jesus is—a church that sloshed grace into a graceless society—then we needed to be willing to risk going into deeper water with Jesus. He was inviting us to go where we'd never gone before; a place where Helen had never gone either. What life were we going to wait for? We were following Jesus out to the risky places where we'd be in over our heads—the perfect place to trust Him and Him alone with no safety nets. To become exactly who He called us to be.

DON'T BE AFRAID

Could it be that Jesus is telling us the same thing He spoke to Peter two thousand years ago?

> Jesus replied to Simon, "Don't be afraid! From now on you'll be fishing for people!" LUKE 5:10

So why is it you need to hear that word from Jesus? What might you be afraid of? What are you clinging to? Peter's hands were clutching his fishing nets, but in his mind the issue was far bigger than that. He was thinking, *This is what I know; this is what I'm good at. I'd better not get too far ahead of myself. I'm just a fisherman . . . it's just who I am.* Sound familiar?

Jesus is in your boat today, trying to disrupt your simple little picture, because the truth is that these nets have you all tied up. You think you'll never make a difference, but He came into your boat today because He sees amazing things ahead of you. He loves you and is eager to take you by the hand to lead you into the adventures that your heart didn't even know to long for.

Maybe you're in the boat, and you're thinking, *Don't take me deeper. I'm almost to the point where my life is manageable.* All the while Jesus is whispering to your heart, "If you want to fish for perch forever, only focused on what's small and manageable, that's okay. I love you. But I've got my eye on you for far more than 'okay'—something more expansive, something eternal. I came to compel you to trust Me and leave your nets behind. I want to lead you into the plans I've always dreamed of, where it's you and Me together in much deeper water than this. That instinct you have for more? I hardwired that into you."

What are your nets, my friend? You don't have to be afraid. Whatever you're clutching isn't worth holding on to and missing out on what Jesus is offering you. I'm convinced to my core that every single day Jesus is inviting people into His grander vision, but most of the time they don't receive *His* great plans because they are clutching their safe, familiar ones.

It doesn't matter who you've been or what you've done—the Holy One is calling you out to new territory with Him, right now. *Go with Him.* Don't let lesser things rob you of the rich plans of God for even one more day. Don't stay in the shallows or on the shore. You weren't made to watch. Let Jesus get in your boat, and your life will never be the same. Just imagine the miraculous breakthroughs, breathtaking resurrections, impossible redemptions you will see as you accompany the Son of God into the uncharted water of your new God-crafted life.

> Don't let lesser things rob you of the rich plans of God for even one more day. Don't stay in the shallows or on the shore. You weren't made to watch.

And as soon as they landed, they left everything and followed Jesus.   LUKE 5:11

It happened only a few weeks after Helen accepted my invitation to share her story. This particular Sunday, just before I was to preach the concluding message of our fall series, Helen sat on a stool on our small stage, took the microphone, and introduced herself the way she had countless times before: "Hi, I'm Helen . . ." But the words that came next changed her life—and ours: " . . . and I'm an alcoholic."

She could've clung to her safety nets and remained hidden, protected in her secret, but instead, she took the risk, got in the wheelbarrow, and shared her entire story of alcohol abuse, hiding, self-medicating, and coping with life through drinking. She was candid, vulnerable, and extremely brave. She laid it all out there, including the way Jesus had met her, given her grace, and helped her walk with Him in sobriety for years!

How did the church respond?

Magnificently!

They showered her with love, grace, gratitude, and honor! This was Quest at our usual loving best! But something more than that happened. Jesus had invited all of us out to this deeper water for a reason! Something beautiful began that weekend. A level of frankness and authenticity was birthed. People began to realize, "If Helen can share her secrets and disappointments like that, so can I." Eventually Helen taught a remarkable multiweek series entitled "Grace & Addiction," where people struggling with brokenness and dependencies began to come out into the light.

Dan, an elder, shared his struggle with pornography.

Sandra told the story of her guilt over her abortion.

Amy revealed her addiction to alcohol.

Danny divulged his secret double life.

And Michael told the story of the affair that almost destroyed his marriage.

These are just a handful of the stories that were shared publicly. There have been many more victories shared in smaller groups, in living rooms or around dinner tables, that have been equally powerful. And each points us to the power of God, who has never dropped anyone.

Several years later God gave me an idea, and eventually Helen, now the Transformation Pastor at Quest, helped launch a new ministry called "The Mat," inspired by the story in Mark 2 where four men carried their hurting friend on a mat to Jesus. There, people can find hope and healing in the places of hurt and defeat in their lives. Today that ministry has grown to serve people in more than fifty different areas of struggle. And it's more than just a Thursday night ministry. On the journey to finding hope, hundreds have found new life in Christ and have helped open the door to a culture of honesty and authenticity for our entire church.

When Helen said yes to the invitation and stepped forward that day, she never could have imagined who would be impacted, starting with her brother, Gordon, who surrendered his spiritual pride and entered into an authentic relationship with Christ. And that was just the beginning. Just ask her children, her siblings, her mother, or her father, who are forever grateful.

People are finding help and hope beyond her wildest dreams.

Peter accepted Jesus' invitation. So did Helen. I believe that Jesus is inviting you to leave your nets and go with Him.

I pray that you will.

LIFE WITHOUT NETS

If you are ever going to get into the wheelbarrow and let God actually take you to risky places, you'll have to be intentional. Most of us could use help getting there. I encourage you to use these steps to help you find traction en route to God's deeper water for your life.

1. *Recount God's goodness toward you.* Name the ways God has blessed you, provided for you. It will fan the flames of trust in your relationship with Him. Recall the specific situations, prayers, and circumstances where you sensed that God was making a way for you, providing for you, protecting you. Become fluent in remembering the ways God has proved His love by keeping you and always getting you safely back to shore.

2. *Identify the safety nets in your life.* What are the manufactured means of safety that you cling to that keep

you from living by faith and trusting God to lead the way for you? What are your man-made mechanisms that provide you with apparent safety and false security? Is it money? The applause of your peers? A measure of success? Routine and familiarity? Comfort and ease? Identify the hiding places in your life and recognize that they war against you trusting God. Believe that He has something better for you in the uncharted places He is taking you.

3. *Tear them down.* Now that you've identified your safety nets, cut them down. No matter what materials your nets are made of—destroy them. You will be reluctant to take action and follow Jesus out into deeper water as long as you remain comfortable in your life. Do you need to tear down nets made of fear? Nets knit together by insecurity, worry, or selfish ambition? Just take the courageous step and get rid of them. Confess, share your story, have the lunch, take the risk, ask the hard question, write the check, make the call . . . whatever you do, take a deep breath and get in the wheelbarrow. That's the only way you'll know the thrill of going to the deep places with Christ.

> Live without nets and trust the One who's never dropped anybody.

The truth is, my friend, if you wait around until you're ready, you'll never get in the wheelbarrow. Live without nets and trust the One who's never dropped anybody. You can't afford to leave another offer on the table. Today is the day to join with Peter and say, "If You say so, I will."

GETTING TRACTION

 REWIND

God will never be remarkable *to* you until you allow Him to do the remarkable *through* you.

DOWNLOAD

But if you say so, I will . . .   LUKE 5:5

PUSH PLAY

Identify the safety nets that are keeping you from trusting God. Tear them down and give them to Him.

Chapter 5

THE GRACE PATH

I REGULARLY HOLD PEOPLE under water.

I do it for a living.

They love it.

Before you contact the FBI to set up a sting operation, remember that one of the perks of being a pastor is that you get to baptize people.

At my church, baptisms are one of the highlights of every season. People stand in a pool of water and tell their unique stories of God's rescue in their lives. They hold nothing back. I've heard stories from strippers and prostitutes, politicians and preachers, addicts and church pros, ten-year-olds and ninety-two-year-olds, black, white, gay, straight, the squeaky clean and the utterly broken. For all the differences in their stories, they each have one thing in common: they all reached a point where they acknowledged that no matter what they had tried, nothing worked. In Christ they found lasting hope. It was His love—poured out on the cross—that won their hearts, forgave their sins, restored their lives, and transformed them from the inside out. Their fresh stories of redemption always bring tears to my eyes. Wise veteran onlookers bring plenty of Kleenex; they just know it's that kind of event.

At a recent baptism service, I found myself celebrating with a young girl who had just been baptized. She was standing there with a quizzical look on her face, not uncommon for someone who had just been dunked for Jesus. The look translated to: *I'm now standing here, soaking wet, before an entire crowd of people in dry clothes, and they're all watching me.* Rather than letting the potential weirdness steal her moment, I stepped closer to her and looked her in the eye.

"Now . . ." I began. She looked up into my eyes, unsure of what was coming next.

" . . . just go be yourself!" I said with a smile.

I don't know if that's what she expected, but that's what she got.

Why did she need to hear that? Because how you start matters.

When people take a big step in trusting God—like giving their lives to Christ or getting baptized—they get fired up that God is encountering them, speaking to them, using them. And right about then, one of the biggest enemies of every Christ-follower enters the room: the performance wheel. You know the wheel, right? It's the voice that challenges us to prove that we're serious, to show the strength of our commitment. So we unwittingly get on board and start to work up a sweat for God.

I see more people than I'd care to count hop on the wheel and, with relentless determination, set out to be as "Christian" as they can possibly be. They aim to out-perform the pope, out-preach the pastor, out-sing the song leader, and out-good the goody-goodies. Like a hamster on a wheel, they get caught in an increasingly exhausting pace, inevitably wearing themselves to the bone. Many never get off.

> More people than I'd care to count set out to be as "Christian" as they can possibly be. It's sad. It's lethal. And it's the archenemy of God's grace.

It's sad. It's lethal. And it's the archenemy of God's grace.

But there is another way—a better way!

LIFE ON THE GRACE PATH

Listen to the words of Jesus as He describes a different kind of life—an invitation to all who find themselves exhausted on the wheel.

Are you tired? Worn out? Burned out on religion?
Come to me. Get away with me and you'll recover

your life. I'll show you how to take a real rest. Walk with me and work with me—watch how I do it. Learn the unforced rhythms of grace. I won't lay anything heavy or ill-fitting on you. Keep company with me and you'll learn to live freely and lightly.

MATTHEW 11:28–30, *THE MESSAGE*

Does that characterize your life right now? Are you living "freely and lightly" with Jesus on the Transformation Adventure? Are you experiencing His "unforced rhythms of grace"? He says, "Come. I will help you recover your life. Walk with Me and work with Me." He is inviting us to spend every part of our complex lives with Him, to walk with Him in our families, in our jobs, at school—all the while being replenished, not depleted. Consider for just a moment the reality that Matthew's Gospel presents. The Savior of the world, the Creator of all that is, the One who spoke everything (including you!) into existence sends this personal invitation: Come away with *Me* and you will recover *your* life.

> Come away with *Me* and you will recover *your* life. This is an intimate call from the One who carefully knit you together in the first place.

This isn't just some broad-stroke concept that a sovereign-yet-removed deity tosses out like a king's decree. This is an intimate call to something extremely personal, sent directly to you from the One who carefully knit you together in the first place. It's an invitation to do what only you can do—*be yourself*—walking with Jesus on your Grace Path, in the rhythm of who Jesus made you to be. Not someone else, not performing, not striving. It's living in step with the gifts, passions, skills, and grace God Himself knit into you. The path is traced out by the finger of God—*your tailor-made Grace Path!*

What's the key to life on your Grace Path? Embracing the grace of God every single day.

Grace. It's the amazing, unmerited favor of God; undeserved kindness, overflowing love and generosity. It is the inexplicable expression of God's heart of love for His priceless child—*you*! So embrace it every day.

Grace. "Amazing grace, how sweet the sound . . ."

But if it's so amazing, why don't we *immerse* ourselves in it?

Just like you never want to leave an amusement park, you never want a great movie to end, you never want to see the fireworks at Disney World because it signifies the end of a great experience, we ought to want all of the matchless grace of God we can get. It's so remarkable that it just seems to follow that we'd each reside in it, submerge ourselves in His breathtaking grace that goes on forever and ever.

Yet oddly enough we don't avail ourselves of its endless supply. We do not appropriate it every day and sink the roots of our lives down deep into it. We usually treat it more like fine china that we store neatly away in the hutch, awaiting the perfect occasion to use it. Unfortunately, that occasion never seems to arrive. His grace is left undisturbed

> Sadly, we spend years and years appreciating grace, singing about it, but not experiencing it!

in our lives. Sadly, we spend years and years appreciating grace, singing about it, but not experiencing it! Not only do we deprive ourselves of the freest, most plentiful, inestimable gift of heaven, but we withhold it from others. We treat this beautiful present with a scarce spirit, even extreme frugality, though it doesn't cost us a dime.

WHAT FUEL ARE YOU RUNNING ON?

Point of clarity: I did *not* say that we need to embrace God's grace *just* so that we can be saved and born again. Now, grace *is* the singular way to be born again. The Bible tells us the way we are rescued from sin is by crying out to God for His saving grace (see Romans 10:9; 1 John 1:9). You ask Him to forgive your sins, invite Him into your heart, and then surrender to His leadership all the days of your life no matter what the cost. You throw yourself on the mercy of the court.

Grace is how it all begins.

But where does it usually go from there?

After we receive the grace of God, our sins are washed clean and we are made new. You say "Amen," perhaps someone gives you a Bible, maybe you even celebrate with a free lunch from your friends. But here's where the detour begins: you decide, *I'm gonna behave like nobody's business.* It means no more sinning (at least in those big ways), developing a rigorous Bible reading plan, and asking God to bless you along the way.

But guess what? Even though it sounds noble, that's not the Grace Path!

How many people say they were saved by grace but then live by sheer willpower and grit?

You were designed in your core to live every day by God's grace! It's how you are supposed to approach each day of every year for the rest of your life. You don't become a Christian through performance and effort, and you aren't meant to live that way either. Instead, you admit that you don't have the power to be humble, tender, or generous, to love your neighbor, or to care for the poor. Daily you come before God saying, "I come to You for grace. By the power of Your Spirit, You can transform me. You can accomplish what I cannot." It's a prayer He's eager to answer, because He loves you too much to let you live on your own willpower. Grace is the premium fuel you're meant to run on.

I was given a timely illustration to help us learn this. I'd taken a few days away to spend time writing this book; things were going well, and after a particularly long day of writing, I invited some friends out to dinner for a much-needed break. After a great evening together laughing, hanging out, and eating delicious cheesecake, we piled in my truck. As we drove home a little later than we'd planned, we pulled over to get some gas.

> God loves you too much to let you live on your own willpower.

My crackerjack assistant, Dani, hopped out before I had the chance, got the pump going, then got back in the truck.

I don't know if it was the lateness of the hour or if there was a full moon that night or what, but from that point on, things did not go according to plan. As we sat and waited for the tank to fill, we continued to tell stories and have a blast. Suddenly, Dani jumped from the truck when she heard the gasoline start to spill out of the gas tank—the autostop hadn't worked! As I looked up to see Dani grabbing the nozzle, my focus shifted to the green sign behind her head. *Diesel.* My heart sank.

"Dani, you did *not* just put diesel in my truck, did you?" I yelled.

Panicked, she looked over her shoulder at the sign.

"YES!" she shouted. "Yes, I DID! What do we do?"

I leaped out of the truck. Yep, it was true—25.2 gallons of prime diesel fuel were sitting in a tank designed for only unleaded. Over the course of the next *four* hours (involving three YouTube "how-to" videos, one borrowed car, a midnight trip to Walmart, a hand pump, and three Marlboro-smoking "Good Samaritans") we slowly, painstakingly, siphoned 25.2 gallons of diesel from my truck. Every person we encountered throughout the entire night's adventure had the same cringed-face response:

"You did WHAT? *Diesel?* Ooooooh . . . that's *BAD*. You may have totally ruined your truck!"

When we use the wrong fuel, bad things happen. Thanks to Charlie, Josh, and Ben (and a YouTube video from Doug), my truck's okay. Dani still has her job. I maintained my sanity. We caught it in time. No lasting damage done.

But if we had driven just a couple of miles down the road with diesel in my truck, you'd be reading a different ending to this story. The engine would have been completely destroyed.

Some people live their whole lives running on the wrong fuel, and while it may not happen immediately, over time, their engines break down. *They* break down. And they stall out on the side of the road instead of soaring along the Transformation Adventure that God has for them.

If you fill your tank with willpower and effort, you'll burn out, and ironically enough, you will likely blame God when it happens. You will reason that Christianity just didn't work for you. Yet what you are calling "Christianity" is miles away from what Christ intended. He never wanted you to accept the performance wheel's lethal invitation in the first place. God's intent has always been that you would run on the fuel of His grace along the path He crafted for you.

> God's intent has always been that you would run on the fuel of His grace along the path He crafted for you.

SHARON: BECOMING HERSELF

You can't start a church alone. It takes great people to build a great community. When I was stepping out with Jesus to launch Quest Community Church, one of my continual prayers was for Him to point me to high-capacity people who shared my love for His bride and for those far from God. I was praying for like-minded people to join my small team and give 110 percent in a pioneering effort to do nothing less than change the world.

Sharon was exactly who I was looking for. She had all the qualities I was searching for and more. This former "School Teacher of the Year" was a brilliant, talented, entrepreneurial person who could sing, teach, and lead like nobody's business.

But there was a problem. She didn't know or see any of that in herself.

While Sharon loved Jesus, people, the church, and the mission God had called us to, she had no real clue what she was capable of, or that she was designed to make a difference. She had devised her own plan and set out to fulfill her own little dream for her life. Sharon was a devoted mom raising great kids, a terrific wife making a wonderful home for her and her husband, Paul. The path Sharon had chosen could essentially be boiled down to being "a nice, sweet Christian woman."

The trouble with that was clear: I had a hunch that Sharon was made for more—much more. Like a coach who sees an untapped skill or a teacher who sees a mind not being stretched, God saw far more for Sharon than she saw for herself. She was made to rescue spiritually lost people. She was designed to lead thousands in becoming awe-inspired worshippers of Christ. She was crafted to lead scores of people into the loving arms of Jesus. He had rescued Sharon to be a forcefully advancing leader in the only endeavor on the planet charged with expanding heaven and shrinking hell. She was about to push play and become herself—and I couldn't wait to see her step into it.

When I approached Sharon about joining my team, she was stunned that I even wanted her help. She reluctantly agreed to a six-month trial run to see if it fit in the rhythm of her carefully crafted, self-made life.

I'll never forget saying that first, conditional yes. While I felt the pull of a "normal," safe life for me, my marriage, and my kids, I could not deny the voice of God propelling me to step forward into the potential life He had for me. My fear was pretty simple: Would my kids be okay if I wasn't there every minute? What would happen if I stepped out of the safety of the American dream of a life I had so carefully shaped and stepped into the unknown? While I didn't have all the answers, I knew the heart and character of the One who was calling me out, and I said yes. Was I scared? Yes. Was it worth it? Absolutely.

It didn't take long before God began to reveal His heart for me and my family. Risk by risk, step by step, I began to experience the truth that what my kids needed most was a mom who was trusting God—living in the palm of His hand. And as we trusted Him, God was faithful; and soon, the most beautiful thing started to happen: my kids started to see that trusting Jesus uncondition- ally is the new "normal" and that living in risky faith territory is the freest place to live. I can't believe what He

*has done in us . . . in me. It turns out that everything
comes to life as we trust the One who is always faithful.*

Within the first month, Sharon Clements discovered who
she was made to be. While living a small, faithful life dedicated
to your family, your plans, your projects and dreams can be
sweet, Sharon wasn't made to be sweet. God's Grace Path for
Sharon wasn't a small, self-absorbed, innocuous life. She was
made to explode with gratitude, lead with grace, and reach out
with irresistible passion. This was how Jesus designed her, how
I saw her, and who she now saw herself becoming.

Fifteen years have passed since Sharon missed her six-
month trial window. She's now the senior leader on my staff.
I've had a front-row seat as she has gone from self-absorbed
mom to world-class leader. Most recently, I've enjoyed watching as she leads The Uprising—a ministry that challenges
and equips thousands of pastors around the world to step
into their Grace Path and become the world changers Jesus
has called them to be—just like she did. As long as Sharon
continues to be herself, the cause of Christ will continue to
flourish in her life.

LANDMARKS ALONG THE WAY

Each person's journey is different, but there are common
markers along every Grace Path. Many of these components
surface in the form of newly germinating seeds when we
first come to Christ. While they wither on the performance

wheel, they blossom on the Grace Path. Sharon's life shows us that what started as just a hint can grow and take on full expression as God's power is released through our agreement.

In Jeremiah 29:11, the prophet writes,

"For I know the plans I have for you," declares the LORD, "plans to prosper you and not to harm you, plans to give you hope and a future." JEREMIAH 29:11, NIV

When we're living out the plans of God for our lives, we sync up with Jeremiah 29:11, and certain unmistakable indicators begin showing up in our lives as natural by-products. They may not all be present and active all the time, but for our purposes, I'm listing eight of the most common landmarks I've noticed that point us toward what life on the Grace Path can look and feel like.

Confidence

One of the first characteristics I observe in those of us who take this route is an emerging confidence that we are being the people God made us to be. It may not be who our in-laws want us to be, it may not be about being better than our siblings, it may not mean we are the most popular, and it may not guarantee us any earthly prosperity. But there is a solidity of spirit and a core confidence that we're finally being who God designed us to be; we're comfortable in our own skins for the first time. We are becoming ourselves.

Humility

When we are in the zone, it's not hard to sense a deep and life-giving humility growing within us. It emerges as we gain an increasingly clear picture of who we were before Jesus rescued us. Humility allows us to recognize the beauty of being rescued and the magnificent power it took to accomplish that. God's love, Jesus' sacrifice, and the gift of limitless grace compels us to worship the One who went to such lengths on our behalf.

Gratitude

Not unlike humility, gratitude becomes a marking characteristic in the life lived on the Grace Path. When we consider the vast extent of God's transformational work in our lives, our jaws drop open. There is very little room to be presumptuous in light of all He's done. It becomes unmistakably personal: God loves *me* enough to send His Son for *me*, enough to pursue *me*, enough to die in *my* place? When we truly grasp all that our great God did to win our hearts, gratitude wells up and spills out of us. We did so little. He took extreme measures. We are the recipients of a divine miracle, and we are grateful.

> There is very little room to be presumptuous in light of all God's done.

Joy

Those of us on the Grace Path have a difficult time containing our newly emerging joy. On the one hand it can be attributed to the miracle of God's redemption. He has given us a new heart (see Ezekiel 36:26) and a fresh start (see 2 Corinthians 5:17). We now find ourselves motivated and excited to put our hands to the things that seem tailor-made just for us to do. We once found happiness in self-advancement and self-centered endeavors. Now our hearts race when we advance the cause of Christ. The things that make His heart race ignite our own. We are not only sensing the smile of God in our day-to-day endeavors, but those around us experience the overflow of our fruitful lives. Joy grows where frustration and resentment used to reign. We are walking the road God has designed for us.

Peace

Those of us walking the Grace Path discover that what was once elusive and fleeting now resides deep inside of us. When we have bad days, seasons, even years where nothing seems to be turning out as we would choose, there is an unshakable peace flowing through us because we know we're still on God's path. Even in times of struggle or disappointment, we can rest in a deep and abiding sense that God is close at hand as we follow Him through life. When life isn't predictable or comforting, the God who loves and claims us as His own *is*! Our Transformation Adventure isn't marked by striving or straining after some elusive golden ring; there is a constant peace that His presence brings. On the Grace Path it is clear that Jesus keeps the promise He made in John 14:27: "Peace I leave with you; my peace I give to you" (NIV).

Freedom

On the Grace Path—*we are free!* When we're off the Grace Path, we feel the pressure to measure up, to behave like, look like, sound like exemplary Christians. On the path, that burden is lifted, because we are on the road that the finger of God is tracing out. It is forged out of what Christ has already done, not what we'd better continue to do. Freedom abounds as we live for an audience of One, recognizing that He alone is our example, our leader, our judge. Being a Christian isn't a popularity contest. It's a relationship of irrevocable intimacy with the God who never changes His mind and promises that nothing will come between you and His love. Now that's real freedom!

Attractiveness

When we are living on our Grace Path, there's an undeniable magnetism that emerges. We no longer live for the approval of the people around us. There is something strong and solid in us as we live fruitful, growing lives. People are often intrigued and drawn in as they observe us. There is nothing as contagious as men and women who have discovered who they are in Christ and what He made them for. People on their Grace Path are among the most contagious people you'll meet.

> When we are living on our Grace Path, there's an undeniable magnetism that emerges.

Favor

Have you ever known someone who always seems to be experiencing God's blessing? Someone for whom things tend to break in their favor, as if the smile of God is continually upon them even in the midst of challenging circumstances? The lives of those on the Grace Path tend to reek with the favor of God. His favor comes as we spend our lives in sync with the purposes and plans of God. He blesses and brings effectiveness to what we put our hands to. It is here that increased influence and enlarged borders come into play. Read about Joseph in Genesis 39 to see a breathtaking study about a man who lived in the favor of God even when circumstances were difficult. God's blessing and favor are kissing cousins; where you find one, you'll find the other. It's the unmistakable signature of the Grace Path.

LIVING IN THE ZONE

One of my favorite parts about the Grace Path is that one size does *not* fit all. You heard me right. Someone else's Grace Path won't fit you, and yours won't fit anyone else.

God has a specific, custom-fitted Grace Path just for you.

So how do you know when you're on it?

It's going to take the unique power of football to explain this.

When my son, Corey, was in eighth

> God has a specific, custom-fitted Grace Path just for you.

grade, he had what analysts and sportscasters would call a "career game." Honestly . . . no dad-exaggerating here. In one game, he scored three touchdowns from three different positions. If you're not a football fan, just believe me, that's almost unheard of.

As we were talking about the game at the victory celebration, Corey asked, "What if I did that again, Dad?" Looking at the rest of the season in front of him, he saw opportunity.

I saw something different—a teachable moment.

"Son," I said, "it's called a 'career game' because it's not something that's likely to happen again."

He dismissed my fatherly wisdom with a look that said, "Come on, Dad. Give me a break."

So I responded, "Let me teach you a lesson. I'll put my money where my mouth is. If you ever do this again, I will give you $100 in cash."

It didn't take many games until the little overachiever did it again. My new iPhone wallpaper? Corey holding up three fingers (one for each touchdown) with a huge smile and a look on his face that says, "I told you so!"

After paying up, I encouraged my budding entrepreneur, "Okay, forget my teaching moment and your earning potential. Just do your best and have a blast."

I intentionally didn't bring up any mention of rewarding him if he ever had another career game.

By the time the play-offs came, Corey was riding high on an incredible season. I remember watching the game, thinking, "He's making this look easy." He was in the zone. You could have convinced anyone watching that he was two years older than the other kids he was playing against, but that wasn't the case.

As he scored another touchdown, some friends watching the game with me leaned over and asked, "Are you going to have to pay him another $100 if he gets a third?" I laughed it off. *If Corey does score again, there's no way he'll remember our little deal from earlier in the season.*

Just at that moment, Corey looked up at me in the stands and started counting out invisible dollar bills!

When all was said and done, it turned out to be a *four-*touchdown game.

Best money I ever spent. I was so proud. Broke, but proud!

When you're in the zone, you are decidedly yourself. There's a sense of rightness, like you belong there. What's difficult and cumbersome to others comes naturally to you, like Sammy Hagar and Eddie Van Halen making music that never ceases to rock, like Bob Carlisle hitting notes that make Jesus stand and applaud, or like my funny friend, Adele, who can't sing a note but makes me laugh even when I probably shouldn't. There's a joy, ease, and freedom that come along with being in your zone.

Life "in the zone" is a lot like life on the Grace Path.

When you are on *your* Grace Path (not someone else's), you feel more yourself than at any other time in your life. You are being YOU—the person God created you to be—and it feels amazing.

THE HIGH STAKES OF THE GRACE PATH

Living on the path God designed for you matters, but not just for you.

Let Sharon's story serve as a reminder and encouragement. She had no idea how expansive the impact of her agreement with God would be, and neither do you.

First Peter 2:11 tells us that those in Christ are "temporary residents and foreigners" in this world. You and I are just passing through. The apostle Peter warns us not to get too comfortable or cozy, because life on planet Earth is a layover on the way to our real home and an unbelievable life yet to come.

So why are we here? Why not just give your life to Christ and get instantly transported to heaven?

The reality is that Jesus gave His life for you, but also for your neighbor, your cousin, your husband, your children, and everyone else you know. He leaves you here to represent Him so that the people in your life will have a shot at knowing Him too. Your Grace Path has very real implications for them because it guides you into *living a life that changes the world*. Walking out the plans and purposes God has for you is essential because as you walk with Him, they see Him in you.

Think of it like this: when we serve God out of an obligatory sense of "ought," we find that we are exhausted and our work is less than fruitful because it lacks the power of our authenticity and the strength of God's favor. When a person walks the path God intends for them, something real, life-giving, and compelling happens. Over time your life ignites *others* to live out the Transformation Adventure *they* are created for. In other words, *your* Grace Path impacts *theirs*.

Walking your Grace Path is revolutionary by nature. It's the way the world is changed one life at a time. You become a beacon, pointing people to a truer, richer life that they have yet to experience and a home yet to come. It's a life and a future they have suspected and desired.

When the reality that this world is not our home gets anchored in our hearts and minds, it begins to change everything. It helps us set our compass for the right destination. It prevents us from veering off route into things that are fruitless and unimportant. It assists in establishing and keeping us on the path that God has set apart for us.

Are you in the middle of doing things right now that God does not intend for you, yet you're asking Him to bless them? He won't do it. You know why? Because He loves you! He won't bless a plan that He didn't pick for you. It isn't for your best. That isn't to suggest that He doesn't bring good things from misguided decisions we make. He certainly does. But why not be the you God intends? It will be you at your best.

In the book of Romans, the apostle Paul writes,

So since we find ourselves fashioned into all these
excellently formed and marvelously functioning parts
in Christ's body, let's just go ahead and be what we

were made to be, without enviously or pridefully comparing ourselves with each other, or trying to be something we aren't.   ROMANS 12:5–6, *THE MESSAGE*

Let's just be who we were made to be! How about, with God's help and your cooperation, you just be *you*? Stop trying to reach the bar set for someone else, designed for someone else. Be the you that God crafted in your mother's womb. He knows every step on your Grace Path. He will reveal it to you and lead you there.

THE TWO PATHS

So what happens if you don't walk the Grace Path?

There's only one alternative: the self-made path.

Crazily enough, it really does come down to just two paths: There is the God-devised Grace Path, and there is the human-devised self-made path. The first was crafted in love as God saw all your days before a single one had come to pass. The second flows from an inflated sense of self-awareness, birthed in a self-centered attempt to control your own life and serve your own best interests.

Does that sound a little harsh or overstated? It's not. Rarely does the self-made path get identified for what it really is. It's just good, old-fashioned sin.

Now, the choices we're making and the shots we're calling don't always seem "sinful." We're just going about our plans and trying to manage our lives for us and our loved ones. But the self-made path conceals a secret: it's not the Grace Path that God designed for you, which means that when you're on it, you are not yourself. You are trying to be someone else. Maybe it's a destination handed off to you by a parent, a friend, a teacher, a coach—likely someone who had a different dream for you. But look closely and you'll see that the self-made path is an ancient road. Its beginnings are as old as humanity itself, and it always has one aim: you and I playing God in our own lives, a role we were never meant to assume.

What characterizes the self-made path? It's exactly the opposite of the life you were made for on the Transformation Adventure.

> I don't believe that the self-made path is the life you want.

While the Grace Path is marked with confidence, you find yourself walking in insecurity and self-doubt. Rather than humility, an elevated view of yourself and other prideful thoughts impede your growth. Instead of being filled with joy, you find yourself resenting those who succeed and do well. You've had fleeting moments of peace but long stretches of anxiety that ride roughshod over your emotions. You are not free; you're trapped on the performance wheel, doing all you can to gain the approval of those around you. Rarely do you experience an overflow of gratitude toward Jesus, who gave His life for you. Instead, you fight jealousy, especially toward those God appears to be blessing. You're not a contagious Christ-follower attracting others to God. Instead, what they see in you leaves them uninterested in

Him. You long for the favor and blessing of God in your life, but instead you feel ineffective and unable to get traction.

So which road are you walking? You get to pick.

THE GRACE PATH	THE SELF-MADE PATH
Confidence	Insecurity
Humility	Pride
Gratitude	Jealousy
Joy	Resentment
Peace	Anxiety
Freedom	Performance
Attractiveness	Ugliness
Favor	Ineffectiveness

Call me optimistic or naive, but I don't believe that the self-made path is the life you want. You want your one and only life to count; you want your life to matter. At some level, you want to honor God and carry out His plans in this world with the one life He's entrusted to you.

If that's true, then the Grace Path is the one you want. And if you're going to walk it out, you're going to need to take some action.

You've got some choices to make.

REPENT OR RESENT

As you take the on-ramp to the Grace Path, there's a step that must be taken before any other: it's called repentance.

It's essential to repent when we've chosen our way

over His. We've got to acknowledge that we've chosen the wrong road, and then "unchoose" it. How do you do that? By heading—and continuing—in the opposite direction. Through that step, humility begins to find its way into our hearts. We grow in our receptivity to God's leadership as He guides us on the Transformation Adventure He made us for. Without repentance and the resultant humility, we find that we end up resenting those around us who are excelling on their Grace Path. We resent the people who have what we don't: the money, the life, the influence, the marriage, the calling, the favor, the *whatever*. We resent it all. I've seen it, and it's not pretty.

It's your choice: repent or resent.

I highly recommend that you humble yourself and choose the former. If not, you will live out a small life making little

> It's your choice: repent or resent.

to no impact for Christ. Instead, resentment may well become your defining mark on this world.

The second action you're going to need to take is to develop a holy hatred for the self-made path. You must become uncomfortable with the thought that you are the one who knows what's best for your life. The truth is: Jesus knows and you don't. Our first step is to acknowledge that, left to our own devices, we tend to make decisions that are self-absorbed, often based on self-preservation and comfort. It's not in our basic nature to be humble and to admit our need for help and guidance, much less to be suspicious of our own perspective. But as King Solomon writes,

There is a way that seems right to a man, but in the end it leads to death.   PROVERBS 16:25, NIV

When we admit this, believing that He indeed knows the right path for us to follow, we begin to trust the One who knows best and to stop assuming God's role in our lives. It's in following the direction of the One who wants only the best for you that you will find yourself walking with a new sense of strength and confidence as He leads you down the path of freedom and life. It's an every-single-day process, and these are the early steps on your Grace Path.

Third, you're going to need to admit that there are things at which you don't excel. And you need to be okay with that. You aren't good at everything. News flash: you aren't good at *most* things. But you are able to do what you're called to do—it's the promise of God (see 1 Corinthians 12; Hebrews 13:21; Ephesians 2:10). Identify what you're *not* lousy at. Begin with the question "What am I good at?" That's a great early step in your life on the Grace Path.

Confession time.

I have done some things I was not good at. When I was in seminary, part of the curriculum required a certain amount of time serving in a local hospital as a chaplain. As a future pastor, attuned to the heart of God and sensitive to people's pain, it should have been a piece of cake, right?

I was horrible at it.

Nothing about it fit. Typically when chaplains are called, there is a certain amount of chaos happening. I would arrive on the scene in a hospital room, only to find nurses and doctors rushing around a suffering patient. Sometimes there was blood, and it was not pretty.

But the chaplain is here now—the spiritual leader on the scene. Everything should be fine, right?

I wasn't sure what to say or what to pray. Here's the basic content of my prayers as a chaplain: "God, either heal this person or take them home! They look horrible and sound even worse. Amen!" I would counsel the doctors, "Hey, doc, I think you might need to let this dude go—he looks awful!"

I was a terrible chaplain.

How about we make a deal? Let's both admit that we are bad at some things and never try to do them again. Jesus has plenty of people that He gifted with a certain set of skills for their Grace Path—let's let them do it!

So what are you good at? What gifts and passions has He given you? What are you wired for?

Are you a strategic thinker? Help is needed in
    organizing and advancing the ministries in your
    local church.
Remember those guitar lessons you took in high school?
    There may be a spot for you on your church's
    worship team.
There are suffering people at your local hospital who
    need your encouragement.
Does your heart break for those suffering in

compromised situations? Your compassion may be the answer to someone's prayer.

God has given you a generous heart so your finances can be used to help others.

Your heart for teenagers is needed in your church's youth group.

Has God wired you to offer encouragement? Your pastor needs it.

It's high time you identify and invest in the gifts and passions God has given you. You are way more needed than you know. Get on the Grace Path and turn your back on the self-made path.

You won't believe how good it will feel to be in your zone, doing what God made you to do. Jesus says, "Come away with Me. Learn the unforced rhythms of My grace. Quit performing. Then you will really rest. . . . You will live freely and lightly."

The Grace Path He has for you is exactly what you're looking for.

Now just go be yourself!

GETTING TRACTION

REWIND

God has a specific, custom-fitted Grace Path just for you.

⬇ DOWNLOAD

Are you tired? Worn out? Burned out on religion? Come to me. Get away with me and you'll recover your life. I'll show you how to take a real rest. Walk with me and work with me—watch how I do it. Learn the unforced rhythms of grace. I won't lay anything heavy or ill-fitting on you. Keep company with me and you'll learn to live freely and lightly.
MATTHEW 11:28–30, THE MESSAGE

▶ PUSH PLAY

Take fifteen minutes and identify whether the fuel you're running on is coming from the performance wheel or God's Grace Path for you. Make a plan and get off the wheel.

Chapter 6

REALITY CHECK

HAVE YOU EVER BEEN to the doctor and received a report you weren't expecting? Maybe something serious or concerning? Right after that news, what you want to hear your doctor say is, "It's treatable." Perhaps they send you home with medication, maybe an exercise or treatment regimen, perhaps a diet shift. If you work the plan, they tell you, the plan will work.

But sometimes the report comes with news you don't want, a disclaimer you don't want to hear: "This is something you can *control*, but there's no cure."

That's biology.

When it comes to our spiritual lives, that's an unacceptable diagnosis. Some things were never meant to be controlled or managed—they were meant to be defeated and conquered, permanently.

Right now, I'm talking about *insecurity*.

Insecurity. It started with labels we were given long ago, perhaps rooted in some element of truth, that have taken on inordinate power in our lives. Over time, they grew into an impressive library of condemnation and accusation.

No one makes us read the books—we choose to. Over and over again we recite, relive, and replay them in our minds. It takes so much energy. Instead of going about the business of living the life God created us for, we are stuck in the past rather than advancing on our Transformation Adventure.

If I'm describing the inner workings of your own heart and mind, you are not alone. Insecurity has become a pandemic. Despite how rampant, damaging, and pervasive it is, most of the time insecurity flies under the radar—sometimes masquerading as pride—silently eroding the confidence of millions.

In one of the best frontal assaults on insecurity I've ever seen, author Beth Moore tackles this killer in her ground-breaking book, *So Long, Insecurity*. While dismantling the lies undergirding insecurity, she also writes about the truly insidious nature of this enemy: "You can overcome it. But don't expect it to go quietly."

Let me offer you this definition so that we can name our enemy for what it truly is: Insecurity is a profound sense of self-doubt, a feeling of uncertainty about your worth, the voice that second-guesses your choices, your feelings, and your value. This sense of self-doubt acts as a lens covering our senses, corrupting reality, and distorting what we see in the mirror. The reality might be one thing (and obvious to everyone around you), but the lens of insecurity leads you to believe something entirely different. When someone speaks words of value and truth to you—"I love you," "You're valuable to me," "You're the one I've always wanted"—you don't hear it from a pure place. Subsequently, you don't believe it or receive it. You hear it, but you don't trust it. You refuse to take their words at face value as intended. You may nod and smile, but you don't believe it in your heart. What you see in the mirror gets distorted, what you hear in your ears gets twisted, and you believe nothing is pure, accurate, or true.

> Insecurity is a profound sense of self-doubt, a feeling of uncertainty about your worth, the voice that second-guesses your choices, your feelings, and your value.

AN INTERNAL ASSASSIN

It reminds me of a reality TV show I came across recently. The creators of the show gathered together a group of people to be sent out to interview for a job, buy a car, or accomplish some other ordinary task. But before being sent out, they had a date with professional makeup artists, who painted ultrarealistic scars onto their faces. After spending time in the makeup chair, participants viewed their new scars in the mirror and then were sent on their way.

Returning from their various tasks, the participants were interviewed about their experiences. To a person, their answers were almost identical: "It was so awful," "People were staring," "We could sense their judgment," "They didn't treat us normally," "I don't feel that I got a fair shot." Only after they had shared the trauma of their experiences did the producers reveal what was really going on. After the participants had seen their scars in the mirror, the makeup artists had made one final adjustment: *they had actually wiped away the scars.* The participants' experiences, though real to them, weren't rooted in reality. They all went about their day, looking completely normal, but assuming that no one saw them as attractive, respected, or capable.

Some of us walk around like that—like there is something wrong with us that everyone knows about. We assume that people know what we did, that they know our flaws, our weaknesses, and that they see them as clearly as scars. Regardless of reality, we decide to just live with it. We let the voice take up residence in our heart of hearts: *People say nice things, but they don't mean them. Deep down, I know what they're really thinking.*

Insecurity drives you to become someone else, to mount the performance wheel, to compare and contrast yourself with everyone, and ultimately to harbor envy and jealousy— all because you lug around a hideous "scar" that everyone sees. All the while, you secretly believe that if you can outearn or outperform everyone else, perhaps somebody will think well of you—at least well enough to ignore the scars.

But none of it is real. It's all the insidious work of insecurity—whispering, accusing, condemning, and internally disfiguring us. In the shadow of insecurity, every compliment, expression of value, or relationship is held hostage by invisible chains.

I remember getting schooled in how pervasive the voice of insecurity can be when I sat down with my girlfriend, Jacki (now my beautiful wife), at the local Denny's. (I know . . . it's true. I'm a big spender.) Despite the fact that we'd been happily dating for several years, I was beginning to notice a disturbing trend. I would compliment her, and she would receive it—sort of. I would tell her she was all I wanted in a girl, that she was beautiful, that I loved her with all my heart, and while she wanted to believe it, it wouldn't sink in.

> In the shadow of insecurity, every compliment, expression of value, or relationship is held hostage by invisible chains.

When I uncorked the frustration I felt over this repeated experience, it got uncharacteristically tense between us. I remember saying, "How in the world can we spend our lives together if you're not even going to believe me when I share with you how I truly feel? If you won't believe it, we don't stand a chance of making it." It didn't matter how many times I said it, wrote it, sang it, or rapped it (which was only once, to be honest). She wasn't disagreeing on the outside—it just wasn't getting very far on the inside.

Am I telling your story?

Are you simply "testing out" the words from people who love you through the lens of insecurity? When insecurity has a hold on you like that, you're tempted to blame others, looking around for your assailant, thinking, "Who did this to me?" But there's no enemy lurking around the corner and nobody to point a finger at, because *we* are the perpetrators of our own bondage. We hold the keys to our own prisons.

And since it's an assassin working from the inside out, it never sleeps. It will always war against love and against steps of intimacy, whether relational, spiritual, or emotional. *Insecurity is intimacy's biggest enemy.* No matter who or what gets close to your heart, insecurity stands on the inside engaged in an active, ongoing monologue: "Not another step. Don't let them get any closer; they'll hurt you. They don't know you're not worth it! Don't believe them or listen to them." This attack on intimacy doesn't just affect your relationship with the people closest to you. Ultimately it impacts your most foundational relationship—it handicaps the growth you want to see occurring in your relationship with God.

> Insecurity is intimacy's biggest enemy.

I KNOW THE ONE IN WHOM I TRUST

It seems like reality for many of us. But what if we didn't take it anymore? What life are we waiting for to make war on the destructive voice of insecurity? What if we were to operate in a different kind of reality, such as the kind the apostle Paul writes about?

> I know the one in whom I trust, and I am sure that
> he is able to guard what I have entrusted to him until
> the day of his return. 2 TIMOTHY 1:12

As he wrote that sentence, Paul's life was a wreck of circumstances; in fact he would soon be killed for Christ. In the face of that reality, he simply declared, "I'm okay with all this. You know why? Because I know the One in whom I trust. I *know* Him; therefore I've learned to trust Him reflexively, even when circumstances beg me to distrust Him. I'm aware that even though my eyes perceive one thing, He is greater than my vision. He created language and listening in the first place; therefore He's greater than what my inner ear is hearing. Since He's always trustworthy, I'm going to rest in Him: I know the One in whom I trust."

If you're tempted to dismiss the example because it's the "great apostle Paul," don't do it. The circumstances were very real—dare I say, more threatening than any circumstances you or I stand to face. But Paul knew that God was truer than his circumstances were frightening. Even in light of these facts, the trust that Paul displayed, while remarkable, was based in Someone more remarkable still.

That same great God stands ready to help ordinary, everyday people like you and me to trust Him, the One who is anything but ordinary. This isn't essentially about us. It's about Him and our choice to believe that He is more than enough.

I still remember the first time I saw Elizabeth's face. Simply put, it was dark. Her eyes were covered by dangling hair, her demeanor was sad and withdrawn, her words were few. She absorbed the energy of those around her like a vacuum. She sat at the end of our long table of twenty-five people at Logan's that Sunday after church. Little did she know this was the beginning of a gorgeous Transformation Adventure.

> For as long as I can remember, I felt like I was constantly being watched by others. This translated to my life as a need to be impressive, no matter what I was doing. Anytime I fell short of perfection, I played the event over and over in my head and internally beat myself up. The same tendency led to a craving for control. When I felt out of control, I subjected myself to mental and physical pain. And I subjected those closest to me to unpredictable mood swings where I lashed out through yelling, slamming doors, and isolation.
>
> By the end of college, I was diagnosed with depression, anorexia, and an anxiety disorder. In an attempt to gain control, create a sense of security, and cope with how disgusting I felt, I alienated myself from my friends and family to order my life around starving, compulsively exercising, cutting, and micromanaging as much of my life as I could. I went to an inpatient treatment facility for

*eating disorders in Arizona twice—the first time for 72
days and a second time when I spent a month and a half
on a feeding tube. I remember sensing God's presence
around me, but it never stayed.*

*A little over a year after I returned home from Arizona,
I had a series of conversations that helped me see who Jesus
really is. On February 12, 2006, I encountered Jesus at the
cross and received Him into my heart. Since that day, I
have been learning what is true about me because I belong
to Him. God, who makes all things new, is redeeming the
years of brokenness. I am not dying anymore; I am so alive!
I no longer survive in hopes of fading away. I am thriving
as God's daughter! I know that I'm accepted by Him, which
makes me significant, secure, and free. I don't always feel
that way, I don't always operate in those truths, but I know
it's true. And I am growing toward consistently living as the
secure person that Jesus has made me.*

Elizabeth found her secure identity in Christ, and you
can too.

I'm convinced that the last breath Paul took was a secure
one. It was the breath he had breathed in and out since
encountering Jesus in the first place. Before the executioner's
blade fell, he knew that this was part of God's Grace Path for
his life, and in spite of the extremely challenging facts, he was
okay. He was solid in mind and spirit. God's trustworthiness
was stronger than the difficulties of his circumstances.

Imagine that kind of reality—trusting God even if you

can't trust the ones around you. Taking steps toward people without the voice saying, "Go no further." Growing in intimacy even as you sit isolated in a prison cell.

Jesus longs for you to know He never made you to live with scars. He's the One who bears the scars that can set us free. In John 8, He says, "If the Son sets you free, you will be free indeed" (verse 36, NIV).

Did you hear that? Free indeed. Trust Him on that.

A QUESTION OF POWER

To be fair, I don't think anyone *wants* to be insecure.

But people can't just decide under their own power and discipline to think differently. Perhaps you've tried and know just what I'm talking about. Something deeper must take place; something that only God can accomplish in your heart and mind. What you don't do is clench your fist and muster all the internal fortitude you can and say, "You know what? You're right. From now on, I'm going to start thinking secure thoughts. I'm done with insecurity right now, because it's time to be secure. Whew, so glad I read that book!"

Don't do it! I just saved some of you a lot of pain and heartache.

Others of you have already learned the hard way.

There's a popular strain of humanist thinking in our world that tries to convince us that, in and of ourselves, we have all the power we need. It's a nice wish, but it's not grounded in reality. You do not have the power to simply draw a line in the sand and declare yourself secure and confident. A deeper, stronger, more thorough work must occur for transformation and emancipation to be real and lasting.

How do I know that? Because there's a more profound lesson to be learned here than simply defeating insecurity.

No one has *ever* transformed himself or herself into a wholehearted follower of Jesus.

It's not a matter of discipline, like resolving to eat better or work out regularly. While those things do impact your life, nothing you can do causes spiritual transformation.

A person becomes a wholehearted follower through a journey. The process begins by considering who Jesus really is and what He taught. But one day along the way, people choose to entrust their lives to Him. They choose to become followers of Jesus, making Him the Forgiver and Leader of their lives. In that moment, something supernatural occurs. Their sins are erased. They are forgiven and reconciled to God. They are adopted into His family. And now, they are spiritual royalty in the Kingdom of God.

> No one has ever transformed himself or herself into a wholehearted follower of Jesus.

John describes what happens when you open your heart to Christ:

> But to all who believed him and accepted him, he gave the right to become children of God. JOHN 1:12

At this moment of your adoption as a child of God, Scripture tells us that Jesus makes His home inside of you; His Spirit takes up residence in your heart (see 1 John 4:4; Revelation 3:20). And it's not the same heart you've always had; in fact, it's a regenerated heart.

The prophet Ezekiel says it remarkably:

> I will give you a new heart and put a new spirit in you; I will remove from you your heart of stone and give you a heart of flesh.   EZEKIEL 36:26, NIV

Almost sounds like a spiritual heart transplant, doesn't it? Ephesians 1:13-14 tells us those who are in Christ are marked with the seal of the Holy Spirit. As a Christ-follower, you're the recipient of the gift of God—His Spirit in your body. When you give Him your life, He gives His life back to you as a seal guaranteeing your redemption. At the end of all things, He'll look for those who have the mark of the Holy Spirit—the deposit of God living in them.

Need I go on? I haven't even cited the verse that marks the entire Transformation Adventure:

> The Spirit of God, who raised Jesus from the dead, lives in you. And just as God raised Christ Jesus from the dead, he will give life to your mortal bodies by this same Spirit living within you.   ROMANS 8:11

Are you catching this? Is it sinking in?

This isn't just you—it's God with His power working

through you. When you place your trust in Him, He doesn't just prepare you for heaven; He empowers a life He has planned for you right now. No longer do we battle in our own strength, but in His. He lives His life through us as we choose to submit to Him and follow Him who died in our place and now resides in our hearts. It is His strength, His power, and His truth that is brought to bear on the voices and captors that we have inadvertently welcomed into our lives. We are now filled with the same power that raised Jesus from the dead.

> When you place your trust in Him, He doesn't just prepare you for heaven; He empowers a life He has planned for you right now.

WRECK AND REBUILD

Think back to the last time you tried to become a secure person by deciding to think better thoughts. How long did it take for insecurity to roar back in? So why is this any different? Because real change happens when we intentionally refuse to do this under our own power. The same declaration we've made so many times—*I no longer want to be marked by who I was: the mistakes, accusations, condemnation, the people I hurt, the regrets, shame*—now gets backed by Someone with the power to do something about it! Instead of just saying, "I'm moving forward," you move forward as a person who is inhabited by the Most High God with the strength to actually take you places light-years beyond those old voices and memories.

If His Spirit can resurrect a dead person, then He's up to the task of handling whatever might be on life support in you. Your eyes and ears may be unreliable, but if His Spirit is in you, lasting freedom isn't just possible— it's part of your royal inheritance!

> If His Spirit is in you, lasting freedom isn't just possible—it's part of your royal inheritance!

Do you realize that when you gave your life to Christ, it was never His intention to renovate you? You didn't invite Him into your heart for a quick remodel. Jesus' plan was always to wreck and rebuild you from the inside out. He wants to redeem your marriage, not slap a Band-Aid on it. He doesn't want to patch you up with Bible verses, sermons, and songs; He wants to set you radically free. The word *redeem* means to pay a price in order to secure the release of someone; to liberate from oppression or enslavement. In the case of insecurity, you're being redeemed from self-inflicted imprisonment. I know it feels safe and familiar, but it's actually robbing you of your destiny and your intimacy with people and with God.

Lasting freedom is an issue of power. When God redeems you, He does so from the inside out, not with self-help and willpower. No one's guilt is ever erased from the outside in; only the Holy Spirit can do this work in you. He is the only One who casts out fear, filling you with hope and joy. It seems a bit redundant, but it couldn't be more accurate: without His lasting power on the inside, you have no real power within! True liberation comes from the Person who created your insides and now re-creates them.

God alone can erase what has occupied the hard drive of your heart and mind and reformat it with His Truth.

JUSTIN: BULLIED

I remember when I first met Justin. God had directed me to rearrange a regularly scheduled board meeting to speak at a college InterVarsity gathering on a snowy night in January. It turned out that attendance was sparse that night (perhaps because of the weather, perhaps because they were Redskins fans). *What's up, God? Did You really want me to change my schedule for this?* But after five minutes of watching a young, guitar-playing worship leader in a college classroom, I knew *exactly* why God had brought me there. He brought me there for Justin.

Justin started attending Quest, and it became readily apparent to anyone who met him that he was a man of exceptional talent and gifting, designed by God to make a seismic impact.

The problem was, Justin didn't believe that.

He had voices—demons from his past—that lived in his head and told him otherwise. For every word of truth, possibility, and promise that was spoken into him, the voices countered with all Justin *wasn't*. He didn't live grateful enough. He didn't live solid enough. If Justin *really* loved God, the internal accusers said, he would love more, give more, pray more, share his faith more, cry more. Nothing Justin did was ever enough.

The voice of insecurity played with Justin like a piñata, bullying him, hitting him when he least expected it, leaving him swinging, unsteady with every wind that came along.

THE VOICE IN YOUR EAR

Whose voice is in permanent rotation in your heart right now? I know you might hear it in your own voice, but can you look for the older voice that preceded yours?

Is it the voice of your father labeling you as a "disappointment"—the child who never reached his or her potential?

Do you hear your mom's voice saying something careless and hurtful?

> Whose voice is in permanent rotation in your heart right now?

Is it the voice of your boss explaining how you don't impress or measure up?

Or the echo of the kids on a playground who laughed, or made fun, or left you standing when teams were chosen?

Is it the voice of your ex who swore he loved you and then didn't look back on his way out the door?

Is it the stinging words of a well-meaning teacher who told you that you were smart and that your sister was beautiful, not knowing you wanted to be considered beautiful too?

The coach who cut you?

The bully who mocked you?

The Christian who judged you?

What is the voice for you?

The older the voice, the more dominant it is on the inside,

as it has somehow maintained its power over you for years, maybe even decades. Perhaps the words that haunt you most weren't even spoken with bad intentions, but insecurity stepped in as your translator: *I know what they were really saying.*

What are the voices? Can you identify them?

God wants to delete them all.

All of them: the words, the voices, the memories, everything. He wants to displace them in your heart and utterly destroy them. He intends to take the lies, the accusations, the condemnation, the biting failures, the hopelessness, and the isolation, and He wants to redeem your core.

> The operative question is, Will you agree to cooperate and allow Him to do His powerful work in you?

There's no question that God is powerful enough to do this. He began by speaking the world into existence, and He has been rescuing, redeeming, and resurrecting people just like us ever since. If you know Christ, the question isn't even whether you have the power of God within you to see this through. The operative question is, Will you agree to cooperate and allow Him to do His powerful work in you? Then it's time to stand together and make war.

JUSTIN FIGHTS BACK

There's one thing you need to know about my friend Justin: he's a fighter. I'm not sure if that's who he always was, but I can promise you that's who he's become.

You see, throughout his longtime struggle with the debilitating voice of insecurity, he had a deep-seated sense that he was made for something extraordinary. And while the voices of "ought to" and "not enough" made their endless case, there was something deeper, something truer in Justin that rose up. A deeper love for his heavenly Father who had rescued him. A truer desire to see people far from God know the hope and joy he'd found in Christ. A heart after God's own heart that beat to do *everything* Jesus had for him to do with his one and only life. He wasn't willing to go down without a fight.

So Justin made war.

> *I remember the first time I read the description of a "doubleminded person" in James 1:6-8 and realized it was me . . . "a wave of the sea, blown and tossed by the wind . . . unstable in all he does" (NIV). As much as I hated the reality, it was like a diagnosis to a lifelong illness I had never been able to treat. For the first time, it became clear that I couldn't hold God's Truth and my perceptions, feelings, and thoughts about myself as equally true. What I had identified as "me" was riddled with contradictions to God's Word, so much so that voices of condemnation and accusation had become inseparable from "my" thoughts. But simply seeing that didn't change a thing—freedom required confrontations with inner voices that had lived unopposed for decades.*
>
> *During a conference trip with friends at Quest, I began to realize how many of my thoughts were a*

running commentary on the people around me. I would inwardly criticize and pick apart people's words, actions, and motives, being an unintentional accomplice to the voices of accusation and condemnation that ruled over me. After a conversation with a friend on the trip about what I was experiencing, it became clear that to escape the critical voices that dominated my thoughts, I was going to need to expose and confess them for what they really were: sin.

That night, gathered in a small room with the dozen people that were part of our group on the trip, I confessed what I had been thinking and harboring toward other people. It was awkward, embarrassing, and unbelievably humbling to tell them to their faces. But instead of judgment and offense, I was treated with surprising grace, love, and forgiveness. They circled around me and prayed for me, asking God to infuse my heart and mind with freedom and truth. The exposure of these thoughts led to a defining moment of separation from voices of accusation and condemnation. They weren't "my" voice anymore, and for the first time, I began to take aim at the sin and lies that had exercised so much control over my thoughts and feelings.

Step by step, season by season, Justin did violence against the voices that warred against him. He did real battle through prayer. He identified the words that had been spoken, the places he'd agreed, the choices he'd made to become insecurity's unwitting victim. Forgiveness was offered and received; truth was heard and clung to. Justin stopped relying on those old voices to define him and called out to God for His Truth. Friends and mentors prayed for him, counseled him, and called the best out of him. Ground was taken.

Justin fought, prayed, agreed . . . and waited on God to do what only He could do: plant his feet on solid ground.

A QUESTION OF SOURCE

Despite the reality that God redeems from the inside out, we tend to take our formative cues from the outside in.

I've seen people try to base their confidence and security on just about everything you can imagine; so much so, I coined a term to describe our attempts: "temporary confidence shots." When we lean on something external for our confidence, we get a temporary shot of confidence. And I mean "shot"—not a big, tall drink with an umbrella and a straw. A shot—you down it fast and, boom, the thing is gone. There's a reason why consuming temporary confidence shots is so popular and widespread: it works, at least for a short time.

While there's no end to the variety of things people use for temporary confidence shots, I tend to see them break down into three categories:

Appearance

Someone tells you you're looking good since you've been doing P90X, and it lifts your confidence. Perhaps you've had a surgery or a cosmetic change, and people are telling you how great you look. The temporary confidence shot of appearance draws on your looks, your fitness, your clothes, even the impression you make, but it only goes skin-deep.

Competence

Your confidence soars when you're told you understand something better than anyone else. You feel more secure when you accomplish things. There's something so satisfying, at least temporarily, about being seen as competent or "better than." We can derive confidence from our success as a student, an employee, a parent—anything. Your security and your performance are inextricably connected, neither delivering for the long haul.

Acceptance

This shot stems from being seen as part of the "in" crowd. When you were growing up, your sense of confidence skyrocketed when the people you perceived as popular welcomed you into their ranks. When it comes to relationships, it's about having plenty of offers, options, or dates. These shots offer security when you're accepted into the "right" school, when you get the "perfect" job, or when you move into the "nice" neighborhood—but it doesn't last.

What's the biggest problem with temporary confidence shots? It's not that they are so small. Even in small doses, if you could find enough of them, you could potentially live on them (like a steady IV of 5-hour Energy drinks). But here's what we miss: the problem isn't the size of the shot, it's the size of the leak in our hearts.

It works like this: people pour a temporary confidence shot into your life, but before you can even completely digest it, most of it is already draining away. In no time, you find yourself depleted. No matter how many shots you're offered, they leak so quickly that you constantly need the next, and the next, and on and on.

Know why?

Because the circumstances of your life are constantly changing.

You wake up one day to realize that your appearance isn't what it once was. You walk into the room, and you're no longer the rising star. You're shocked. You thought this company would always need you. You thought you'd always be beautiful. But the externals just aren't permanent.

You're the greatest parent in the world; you raised your kids up great. Then all of a sudden, they move from "doing pretty well" in school into a season of intense behavior issues and failing grades.

You gain a little weight, lose a little income, get divorced, have some doors of opportunity close . . . take your pick. What felt like security turned out to be a short-lived booster shot. And when whatever your confidence is propped up on gets rocked, you get rocked. We don't even realize it most of the time, so our solutions are shortsighted: *I need something new . . . to live in a new place . . . to start doing a new thing . . . to get a new car . . . to make some new friends. Then I'll feel better.* But all along, God is whispering to your heart, "You were never meant to base your worth on the externals!"

WHO AM I?

The Gospel of Matthew records a unique moment in Jesus' ministry. Consider the scene. No one really knows who Jesus is. There are a variety of competing theories: prophet, resurrected prophet, recently executed prophet. (Yeah, that last one doesn't make sense to me either, but it was an idea circulating at the time.) Perhaps the prevailing opinion of the day was "Not sure." So much about Jesus was promising, but no one could quite put a finger on who He was.

Suddenly, an ordinary man steps up with another theory. This particular man had no business stepping forward. In fact, every time he did, he tended to put his foot in his mouth; every time he took a step, he sank. Yep, it just tended to go badly for the apostle Peter.

A quick word to those of you who have struggled with a sense of failure in your life: you're in good company. Peter, the right-hand man to Jesus Himself, knows exactly where you're coming from. He's the one you want to sit down with over a cup of coffee and discuss your feelings of failure. There's no gray area with regard to Peter's failures—they are right there in black and white, printed in the bestselling book of all time.

But in a rare moment, he steps forward with . . . the *right* answer! In Matthew 16:15, Jesus asks His disciples, "Who do you say I am?" When no one speaks up, Peter looks at Jesus and says, "Um, excuse me, Jesus? I think I know. You are the Messiah, the Savior, the Son of God."

Silence.

And then Jesus goes nuts!

"Peter! Wow . . . that's *right*! God Himself revealed that to you! Right answer, Pete!"

Peter recognizes the truth about Jesus—a revelation of His identity straight from the mind of God—but he has no idea of the amazing gift that is about to be given to him.

> "And now I'm going to tell you who you are, *really are*." MATTHEW 16:18, *THE MESSAGE* (italics in original)

Can you imagine the scene as Jesus looks into Peter's eyes—the disciple who had been marked by failure and mistakes, the one with more than his fair share of old voices whispering in his ear, the one who tells it like it really is?

"Peter, are you listening to Me? Look into My eyes—you're a rock. I'm telling you who you are, who you really are, Son. You don't have to look at your report card any longer. You don't have to listen to the voice of your dad saying he always knew you'd abandon the family business. You don't have to listen to the Pharisees telling you that you'd better get your act together. You don't even have to listen to the voices in your own head rehearsing all your previous mistakes and disappointments. Look into My eyes, Peter. I'm telling you the truth about yourself: you are the rock upon which I will build My church. You are going to be the first Christian pastor the world has ever known. Thousands are going to have their sins forgiven and their names written in the Book of Life—because of your life! You're no longer a fisherman; you've been approved by the King of kings. Cooperate with Me, Pete. Let Me be the source of your security. I promise you that even when the big blows of insecurity remind you of who you used to be, they'll bounce off and you won't move. Be strong and free. Trust what I tell you, and we will change the world together, My son."

Jesus was right: Peter was a rock. God used Peter to build a church that hasn't stopped advancing in two millennia! Say it out loud as you read: God used Peter to change the world. Say it again, emphatically: God used Peter to change the world!

Do you see where this is going?

The same Spirit that raised Jesus from the dead raised a failure from the ground. In a moment, Jesus simply pressed "delete" on the old voices that haunted Peter. "The power of those voices is gone. I've rewritten your operating system."

> The same Spirit that raised Jesus from the dead raised a failure from the ground.

What would it mean to you if that occurred in your life? What if the voices were silenced? What if you cooperated with God in such a way that He helped you do what Paul prayed you'd do in Ephesians 3:19?

May you experience the love of Christ, though it is too great to understand fully. Then you will be made complete with all the fullness of life and power that comes from God.

What if you put the roots of your life down deep into His love?

"CAPITAL T" TRUTH

I'll never forget August 22, 2005. QCC leaders and volunteers were away at our annual leadership retreat, diving into God's Word and casting the vision for what was next for QCC. I was giving a talk called "God the Great Steward" about living on the solid ground of God's love and His truth as we advance God's church. I asked each person there to accept God's offer to live in the "capital T" Truth of His Word, His voice, His promises . . . and that's when I saw him.

Justin was sitting in the front row, and it was obvious from the look on his face that he had come unglued. God was dealing with him directly. The years of waiting, warring, and persevering were coming together in a moment. God was speaking to his heart words that would change him forever.

"Son, you can put your feet firmly in Me . . . *My* Truth, *My* Love. This is the firm foundation you were *made* to stand on. *Welcome to solid ground.*"

Something broke that day. Justin surrendered to the Truth he was made to build his whole life on, and the old voices lost their power. Something more real and more true broke open in Justin's heart, and he hasn't looked back.

A guy who would rather hide in the background now speaks out with confidence.

A son who used to be unsteady and unsure is now solid and resolute.

A man who was so often in need of a rescue is now a faithful leader and friend who lifts others up every chance he gets.

Justin has become *himself*.

Psalm 40 describes his journey to a tee:

I waited patiently for the LORD to help me, and he turned to me and heard my cry. He lifted me out of the pit of despair, out of the mud and the mire. He set my feet on solid ground and steadied me as I walked along. He has given me a new song to sing, a hymn of praise to our God. Many will see what he has done and be amazed. They will put their trust in the LORD. PSALM 40:1-3

That's exactly what's happened. God took an insecure, unsteady man and planted him on the solid ground of His Truth and Love. And in that place, Justin has stepped onto his Grace Path. He regularly teaches God's Word with disarming authority and has led many to "put their trust in the LORD."

God's Truth will do that to you when you receive it.

I loved watching my seventeen-year-old goddaughter, Carolyne, do just that. She refused to listen to the voice of insecurity that said, "You're just a little girl who likes to sing." After penning her first complete worship song, "Break My Heart," she unassumingly played it for me in the office one afternoon. When I invited her to sing it at an event for seven hundred church leaders, she courageously agreed. It became an anchor for all of us at the three-day gathering and continues to minister to others online.

The beautiful reality is that God is doing this same sort of transformational work in the lives of people every day. I've watched as Alivia has refused to believe that she can't make a difference as she is serving those in our city who have fallen on difficult times by giving them real hope. Her husband, Todd, who had believed the lie that he was insignificant and unworthy, now walks in the truth of God and leads a small group, building strength and confidence into a bunch of men. Brian refuses to wear the scarlet letter of his former hurtful choices. He is now a beacon of hope, bearing witness to the power of repentance, humility, and redemption. You can't look at him and his rescued marriage without seeing the contagious faith he and his wife have in the God of second chances, who rebuilds lives and makes all things new.

When we cooperate with God, we decide to stop counting on that which is temporary and external to give us internal strength. We choose to let God's words shape, solidify, and define us. We decide to receive God's words as "capital T" Truth and stand on that alone. That's the way the words of God displace the condemning, accusing voices in our own heads, no matter how convincing or rooted in "lowercase t" truth they may be. God's Truth always trumps and overwrites the lesser truths that come at us.

So what will it be for you? Whose voice are you going

to give the password to your heart? That night at Denny's, by the power of Christ within her, Jacki began to doubt the voice of insecurity and began the process of learning to stand on the Truth. She chose to exercise trust in God by believing my words and accepting love at face value. That choice untethered our relationship and has allowed us to enjoy over two decades of strong, shared, confident love. Are you going to receive God's Truth and be set free? Or will you continue to be dominated and bullied by the voices on the hard drive of your past that malign and demean you?

I know we've opened ourselves to so many voices—voices that had varying degrees of good and bad intentions, and we've let them stick. Those voices were never meant to have power over you. The only one who wanted to have power over you was the enemy of your soul.

We've been sold some bad information, my friend.

> Will you continue to be dominated by the voices on the hard drive of your past that malign and demean you? Those voices were never meant to have power over you.

You may have actually failed at something, but that doesn't make you a failure.

You may have done some things that are disappointing, but it doesn't make you a disappointment.

Hear the "capital T" Truth of God straight from His heart into yours:

- If I set you free, you are free indeed.
- If I wash you clean, you are pure forever.
- If I make you new, the old is gone and the new has come.
- If I make you Mine, no one will snatch you from My hand.
- If I fill you with My love, you will never be empty again.
- If you cooperate with Me, I'll reformat the hard drive of your life, and you will be remade, reborn, regenerated, redeemed.

"And now I'm going to tell you who you are . . . who you *really* are."

GETTING TRACTION

⏪ REWIND

God's Truth always trumps and overwrites the lesser truths that come at us.

⬇ DOWNLOAD

And now I'm going to tell you who you are, really are.
MATTHEW 16:18, *THE MESSAGE*

▶ PUSH PLAY

Work to identify the lesser voices that are rotating in your heart and mind, and invite God to speak His Truth to overwrite and displace what is false.

Chapter 7

THE CONSTANT

GOD IS LOVE.

It says so in the Bible.

Simple, right?

We've heard it countless times before, some of us have it plastered on a bumper sticker, some of us may even still own colorful bracelets that spell it out. The truth embodied in those three words is easy to overlook, so let's examine it more closely.

The apostle John declares "God is love" in 1 John 4:16. He doesn't say "God *has* love" or "God is *in favor of* love." John puts it plainly: God *is* love; at His very core, the primary quality of God's being is love. I would agree with people who say, "God is holy, faithful, just, and limitless." He is all those things and infinitely more. But John is zeroing in on the foundational reality of who God actually is: "God is love!" Love is the undergirding quality of God that the rest of His attributes stand upon. And since our Great God of love is also the Creator of everything (see John 1:3), He is also the Source of love itself. He is the One from whom all love comes, springs, exists.

God is love.

With that in mind, consider this: the story we see woven throughout the pages of Scripture is one where God has in fact crafted His Creation to be the object of His love. Therefore, when God made you, He created you as *the object of His love*.

Are you tracking with this? The reason you're alive this instant—the reason your heart is beating—is because God made you to love you. How crazy is that? The God of the universe, the Shaper of galaxies and Author of all life, looked into His vast Creation and saw something missing—you.

He made you to love you.

FOR GOD SO LOVED . . .

If you were going to memorize one verse in the whole Bible while on your Transformation Adventure (maybe you're running low on RAM or you just have one of those tiny iPod shuffles that maxes out with three songs), I already know exactly which one I would tell you to memorize. In fact, you might already know it better than you think, even if you haven't picked up a Bible in years.

You've probably seen it at sporting events, on street corners, on billboards, or on a rebroadcast of a Billy Graham Crusade. It's John 3:16—and just in case you've only heard the reference and never known the verse itself, here it is:

> For God so loved the world that he gave his one and
> only Son, that whoever believes in him shall not
> perish but have eternal life.   JOHN 3:16, NIV

For centuries people have discussed how to summarize Christianity, and more specifically, the gospel. I would argue that John 3:16 nails it. There is nothing in the world that matters more to God than you believing and receiving His love. Everything about your Transformation Adventure rises and falls on this fundamental understanding of His love for you. It will serve as the fuel and compass for your journey.

> God made you
> to love you.

God loved the world (meaning the *people* of the world—which includes *you*) so much that He *gave up His only Child*. Let that one sink in a little bit, especially if you're a parent. He gave up His only Son—and He knew in graphic detail what would happen when He gave Him up: the separation, the rejection, the brutality, the crucifixion, a full-on nightmare. Why in the *world* would He do that? So that everyone who believes in Him would not perish.

Stop there for a second.

Let's clarify what the text means by "believe." When the Bible uses the word *believe*, it's different from the way we tend to use it. For example, I can say, "I believe in the Eiffel Tower," even though I've never actually been to the Eiffel Tower. I have no personal, firsthand knowledge of the existence of this impressive structure, but I've seen pictures, I've seen it in movies, and I have friends who have been there. I believe in the Eiffel Tower. But that doesn't really change my life, does it?

Think about it. We believe a *lot* of things: that Michael Jordan is the best to have ever played the game, that Peter Jackson should make as many movies as possible, that the Dallas Cowboys aren't just America's Team—they're *God's* Team.

> What you believe is intended to become a constant— something immovable, unchanging, solid in your life.

But when the Bible speaks of belief, it is speaking of a much deeper reality, a concept that is exceedingly richer and stronger in magnitude. Biblical belief refers to a trust that clings to its object and shapes the actions of a life. Your heart, mind, words, and actions reflect and assume the trustworthiness of what you believe. Biblically speaking, what you believe is intended to become a constant— something immovable, unchanging, solid in your life. That's the kind of belief referred to in John 3:16.

So let's try it again: "God loved people (you and me) so much that He gave up His only Child (Jesus) so that everyone who believes in Him (puts their trust in Christ and clings to Him) will not perish but will live forever (eternally with Him as His children)." Not a bad paraphrase. But here's a quicker way to say it.

God made you to love you . . . *forever.*

He proved it by sending His Son to lay down His life for you. As John says,

> He has given us eternal life, and this life is in his Son. Whoever has the Son has life; whoever does not have God's Son does not have life.   1 JOHN 5:11–12

John is giving us some tough news here: those who are not in Christ aren't really living—not yet. But the great news is that the Son is available to everybody. My friend Zach calls it "the best news." For thousands of years it's been known as the *gospel* (which means "Good News"). In the good news of the gospel, we find this shocking truth: God loves us all so much that He gave up His Son to make a relationship with Him available to everyone.

We blow past this stunning revelation most of the time, so I want us to pause and pay careful attention. I want to share two other verses from 1 John, with my minor paraphrasing to make it more personal. Read it through slowly—in fact, I dare you to go for it out loud.

> God showed how much he loved **me** by sending his one and only Son into the world so that **I** might have eternal life through him. This is real love—not that **I** loved God, but that he loved **me** and sent his Son as a sacrifice to take away **my** sins.
>
> 1 JOHN 4:9–10

Go ahead and tell me how any of that makes sense. What is going on in these verses? What kind of motive would spark God—or *anybody*—to sacrifice the life of their child?

It's clear . . .

God made you to love you.

He was not content just to say it. Words are cheap when it comes to love. He had to show it.

MORE THAN WORDS

I'll never forget the look on Jacki's face.

It was February 14, 1986, our first Valentine's Day as a couple. We had been dating awhile, and we were head over heels in love. I was determined, even as a poor college student, to make sure that she felt it. So I devised a plan: I created a romantic scavenger hunt, placing clues all around campus for her to find. Each clue would guide her to a freshly cut carnation and the next clue.

By the time Jacki had discovered the final carnation, the search had created quite a little buzz on campus, yet she wasn't prepared for the grand finale. Her final clue led her back to her own dorm room, where she discovered a dozen red roses—the first she had ever received.

As everyone on her floor attested, she absolutely freaked out. Her heart swelled. She knew beyond the shadow of any doubt how I felt about her.

When you love someone, you want them to know it.

God so loved us that He was determined to show it. So

He demonstrated what love truly is in the most expensive, extravagant, and expansive way the world has ever seen.

Do you realize what that means? God didn't just *say* it; He wanted us to *experience* it. He isn't content that you believe in His love like I believe in the Eiffel Tower. God wants you to personally know and cling to His love—He wants you to actually *live* in it. The blood of His only Son was shed as proof that He desperately wants you to know His love beyond all doubt and live in the truth of it.

DO YOU KNOW?

As a father, I have felt that same kind of desperation.

When my boy, Corey, was about two years old, we were driving home after a fun day of just being together, father and son. I had one of those clearly cinematic moments (parents, you know just what I'm talking about), where I looked at him in the rearview mirror and was overwhelmed with love for my son. He was simply a little boy, sitting in his car seat, looking out the window. But he was *my* little boy.

As that feeling flooded my heart, I couldn't contain it any longer, and the words just overflowed: "Hey, Corey, you know your daddy loves you, right? You know how much your daddy loves you, don't you?" My heart couldn't have been more on my sleeve—a simple smile from Corey would have completed this Hallmark moment.

But instead of smiling, Corey just continued to stare out the window.

Then, without even glancing at me, he responded in a downright disinterested tone, "No."

"What? What did you say? Are you kidding me?" Silence. This two-year-old had my undivided attention.

Unwilling to relinquish the beauty of this father-son moment, I revised my approach.

"Well, Corey, I was kind of thinking out loud just then, but let me be clear. You do know how much your daddy loves you, right? I'm nuts about you, Core! You must know how much I love you—right, Corey?"

He still wasn't looking at me. Then, in his little boy voice, "No . . . no."

This was going badly. I mean Tony-Romo-fumbling-the-snap-to-lose-the-2006-play-off-game badly. I've got to admit that I was a little rattled. I decided to pull over and actually get out of the car. (I don't know about you, but when I was growing up, if my dad pulled the car over and got out, what happened next was *not* a good thing. But luckily for Corey, I'm a twenty-first century father.) There, on the side of the road, I opened the door and slid in the backseat with him. That got his attention. He turned and looked at me.

"Corey, Daddy's crazy about you, and you've got to know it. Listen, if I could take all the little boys in the whole world and just line them up around the planet, I would walk and walk and walk until I saw your face. I would choose you. Every time. I love you, Son, okay?"

Nothing.

I was officially spurned by a toddler. I had given him everything I had, and he still didn't know how much I loved him! I knew what was next for me—serious therapy. Can you picture the scene? There we are, sitting in the backseat together. I am rocked. He is unconvinced. Our relationship is utterly dysfunctional, and he's not even three yet.

I slowly got out and returned to the front seat. Looking in the rearview mirror at my little spurnster, I decided to try one last time before I started the car.

"Corey, you've got to know this. Daddy *needs* you to know. You need to know. Son, I love you. You really do know, don't you?"

Suddenly, a huge smile lit up his whole face. And as he threw his arms out wide, he yelled with sheer delight, "Dada!!!"

Booyah! Take that, Hallmark.

In one word, Corey was saying, "Thanks for telling me, Dad. I totally get it now. Really appreciate the extra work you went through to make it clear."

We drove home that day, freshly convinced of our great love for each other. And in a new way, I began to understand the heart of the Father who longs for His children to know His unshakable love for them.

A FATHER'S HEART

There's a word in the Bible that roughly translates to "Dada!" In fact, the Bible tells us that we're so adored by God that we're to call Him by this affectionate name; we're invited to call Him "Abba" (see Romans 8:15-16). It's the equivalent of "Papa," "Daddy," or "Dada." He longs for us to call Him by this tender name because we're His children, handmade just for His heart to adore, to lavish with His love.

What if this book, and specifically this chapter, is God's attempt at stopping the car, getting out, and coming around to the backseat? I promise you, it's not to punish you.

He wants to get closer, to look you in the heart and say, "Son . . . Daughter, I love you. I know you might not feel it all the time, but I love you. And I want you to live *knowing* that I love you!" He knows that when you understand that, a smile comes across your face and something shifts in the condition of your heart and soul. Why? Because you know with immovable certainty that your Dada in heaven loves you.

Is that how you relate to God?

> God didn't offer just any run-of-the-mill love. He came in the flesh in the person of Jesus Christ to offer an extraordinary love.

Do you know that the One cheering you on with each step of this adventure is head over heels for you? He adores you no matter what, regardless of who you are or what you've done. No matter the color of your skin, your church attendance, your voting record, your sexual inclination, or your spiritual background, God is nuts about *you*. He just has to think about you and His heart is flooded with feelings of love.

God desperately wants us to know how much He loves us, to feel it to our core. But He didn't just leave it to chance.

He literally got up and came to us where we are—simply to declare His love for us. He didn't offer just any run-of-the-mill love. He came in the flesh in the person of Jesus Christ to offer an extraordinary love that is solid and constant, sacrificing Himself for those He adores.

EXPERIENCE HIS LOVE FOR YOURSELF

Do you *believe* that love?

Better yet: Do you *experience* that love?

The Bible tells us clearly in Ephesians that God's love is not meant to be admired from a distance:

> I pray that Christ will be more and more at home in your hearts, living within you as you trust in him. May your roots go down deep into the soil of God's marvelous love; and may you be able to feel and understand, as all God's children should, how long, how wide, how deep, and how high his love really is; and to experience this love for yourselves.
>
> EPHESIANS 3:17–19, TLB

In light of the fact that God's Word is urging us here to experience His love personally, ask yourself the following question and answer as honestly as you can:

How much do I feel loved by God?

For the sake of simplicity, try one of these possible answers:

I feel it big-time.

I feel it sometimes.

I rarely feel loved.

Be clear: I'm not asking you what you believe *about* His love, and I'm not asking you what you've read. I'm asking you what you *experience*.

As you answer that question, I'm not sure what emotions you might have. We don't often grapple with those kind of experiential questions about love because they're a little risky. You don't ask them in your marriage too often because you're not always sure what you're going to hear. You don't ask them of the friends that matter most to you because it could go badly. If the answer isn't what you'd hoped, the price could be too high to pay.

It's an odd thing to be so mentally convinced of something that you've never experienced firsthand.

Sometimes I run into people who have an odd response to this question. When I ask them how much they *experience* the love of God, they proceed to tell me that they believe that God loves them; they've read it in the Bible all their lives, so they know it. However, they go on to explain that they don't necessarily feel loved or experience His love—they just take it for granted because they assume it's true. It's knowledge, but it has never been experience.

It's like hearing somebody talk about the thrill and the excitement of doing something exhilarating like skydiving.

As they describe in detail how remarkable it is, you realize in the course of your conversation that they've never actually gone skydiving! They know all about it, they've studied it, observed it, have friends who've done it, but *they've* never jumped out of a perfectly good airplane with only a pack and chute on their back. It's an odd thing to be so mentally convinced of something that you've never experienced firsthand.

Or how about this: have you known that you could pay your mortgage but not actually *experienced* the paying of your mortgage? If this happens often, it usually means that you don't actually *experience* what it feels like to live in your house for very long.

When it comes to love, it's incredibly important to know *and* experience it.

So here's the million-dollar question:

What good is a love that is not experienced?

> Your entire connection to God rises and falls on your ability to experience His love for you.

Be it with a spouse, a child, a friend, a family member—and yes, even God—if love isn't experienced, I think you have to begin examining whether you've actually appropriated that love at all. It takes real guts to look closely at that question if you're looking for an honest answer. But it's an essential step in your Transformation Adventure. Why? Because your entire connection to God rises and falls on your ability to experience His love for you.

Remember, He made you to love you.

HE KNOWS WHAT YOU NEED

In one of the most important chapters in the Bible, there's a story that people often overlook. In Matthew 3, John the Baptist has appeared on the scene and is seriously schooling survivalist Bear Grylls on what it means to be a wild man of the desert.

Address? The wilderness.

Diet? Locusts. (I hear they are high in protein.)

Wardrobe? Dead animal skins with a belt (not Louis Vuitton).

Hairstyle: I imagine the just-got-out-of-bed, unwashed grunge look—about two thousand years before its time.

John is on the scene, and in characteristic fashion, he's fighting with the religious establishment, arguing, calling people vipers and snakes; in short, he's not winning any popularity contests, and yet he's unbelievably cool. John is preaching a radical message and baptizing people on the spot in the Jordan River. People are responding in droves; it seems like the height of his ministry effectiveness. And right then, something much bigger happens.

Jesus shows up. And He wants to be baptized.

For thirty years Jesus has been living a rather private life in nearby Nazareth. But a new chapter is about to begin: His public ministry is about to launch. It will be a three-year road that goes from hard to horrific, a road that ends with His gruesome death on the cross.

But this is the beginning. After a brief interchange

between John and Jesus about who should baptize whom, John finally relents and Jesus gets dunked. What comes next is unexpected and unprecedented:

> At that moment heaven was opened, and he saw the Spirit of God descending like a dove and alighting on him. And a voice from heaven said, "This is my Son, whom I love; with him I am well pleased." MATTHEW 3:16–17, NIV

In one of the most supernatural father-son moments of all time, we get a glimpse into the relationship between Jesus and His Dad. The skies rip open, and Jesus hears His heavenly Dada say, "This is My Kid. My Boy . . . My only one. I love Him, and I am fully pleased with Him."

It's a beautiful moment, but you've got to wonder why. Why in the world does God choose to say this to Jesus at this time? Nothing in the Bible indicates that Jesus was unclear on the topic; the Bible tells us that by age twelve, Jesus was already very aware of who His heavenly Father was. What's more, He had spent all of eternity, the previous thirty years notwithstanding, with His Father and the Spirit in perfect unity and community in heaven. But, all of a sudden, the Father now sees fit to offer up this big voice following Jesus' baptism.

Why?

Could it be that for some unknown reason, Jesus needed to experience the Father's love in a fresh way? Could it be that Jesus, approaching this new, difficult chapter in His life, would need to hear and be reminded that His Father in heaven loves Him and is pleased with Him? In light of the challenges ahead, perhaps He needed to hear the indescribable, sustaining, strengthening love that His Dada had for Him.

I think that, for whatever reason, Jesus *did* need to hear it, that He needed to know anew!

If Jesus needed to know, it should come as no surprise that there are times when we also need to hear it anew from our Dada.

Remember, God made you to love you. Beyond that, God doesn't just want you to know you're loved; He wants you to *experience His love for yourself*. He wants your heart to resonate with His voice when He says,

"Dave, I love you. You're My son, and you mean the world to Me."

"Claire, you're My daughter, and I love you; you're the delight of My life."

"Mike, you're My boy. I love you, and I am so pleased with you."

"Jeremy, I adore you, and I've chosen you to be My son."

THE VOICE THAT CHANGES EVERYTHING

When you let this great Truth penetrate your heart, *it changes everything*. Your perspective about life, your perseverance to push through the storm, your patience with other people—everything.

I may not have used your name just a moment ago, but guess what?

God knows your name.

He knows who you are. He knows what's on your mind this second. He knows, the Bible says, what will be on your mind tomorrow. He knows you in every way you can be known because He made you to love you. And He knows how much you need to hear and receive the love and affection He offers you.

I love how Matthew 3:17 is paraphrased in *The Message*. Hear the voice of God—*for you*:

This is my Son, chosen and marked by my love,
delight of my life.

Chosen and marked by the love of God. Is that how you feel?

Living with that kind of experience of God's love is what I call living with a "Matthew 3:17 attitude." It means you're living in the truth of that verse and are confident because of that reality. You know that you are a son or daughter of God to your very core, and that God loves you and is pleased with you.

Some of us have been striving all our lives to gain our father's approval, to make our mom pleased with us, to earn their love. But your heavenly Father cracks open the sky and makes an audible announcement from heaven, saying, "You already have My unconditional love—beyond your wildest dreams." In fact, Jesus Himself wants us to understand that what happened in Matthew 3 wasn't just for Him, but was for us, too.

In John 17:23, He prays to His Father about His disciples (then and now),

> May they experience such perfect unity that the world will know that you sent me and that you love them **as much as you love me.**

When you experience God's love in such a real, true, and personal way, it's no longer just head knowledge; it becomes a life-reorienting heart knowledge.

> I'm not talking about something sappy here; I'm talking about something strong and sturdy you can build your life on.

Now listen all you left-brained people, don't start thinking, *Oh, he's talking to the "feelers."* I didn't say it's a heart *feeling*; it's heart *knowledge*—something you've experienced firsthand. You're certain of it, and as a result, you bank on it, stand on it, swear to it—something that changes everything. I'm not talking about something sappy here; I'm talking about something strong and sturdy you can build your life on.

When you appropriate that kind of love for yourself, there's nothing about you that doesn't get impacted.

Not long ago, a woman approached me after a church service where I had spoken on this topic and said, "Yeah, I remember back when I was a kid, I was baptized. I was glad I did it, but nothing dramatic really happened. I didn't feel any different, I didn't act really different. It was a great experience, but I wouldn't say anything changed about me."

Make no mistake: When the love of God explodes in your heart, things change. Colossians 2:13 teaches us that when we give our lives to Christ, we go from spiritual death to eternal life. That sounds an awful lot like being resurrected, doesn't it? And here's what I know: resurrected people are different every single time. Guaranteed!

I've watched God do the internal miracle of spiritual resurrection again and again. I've heard people say, "I'm sick to death of having just a head knowledge. I want to receive Christ and truly experience His love." While everyone's story is unique, it's unmistakable when the love of Christ sweeps into people's hearts and lives. Later—sometimes months after that moment—they will find me and tell me essentially the same thing: "Everything has changed!"

> When the love of God explodes in your heart, things change.

I remember when Todd, a friend of mine from church, was at the end of a very long journey, processing what it would mean to invite Jesus to come live in his heart and lead his life. After months of spiritual searching and conversations, he revealed to my wife, Jacki, the deeper question burning in his heart: "The truth is, all of my questions have been answered and my barriers to faith addressed. But here's what's holding me back: what if I give my life to Christ and nothing really happens?"

Jacki didn't need a seminary degree to know how to handle this question. She responded with an answer I've seen proven over and over.

"That's impossible, Todd," she said. "It's impossible for the God of the universe to come into your heart and for nothing to change."

She was right: it *is* impossible when you are sincere and genuinely surrender your life to Him. Shortly after that conversation, Todd gave his life to Christ and discovered first-hand that receiving the love of Jesus truly changes everything.

Are you beginning to understand?

God made you to love you. He made you because He wanted a family to love, and He wants you to be part of it.

> See what an incredible quality of love the Father has given us, that we should be permitted to be named and called and counted the children of God!
>
> 1 JOHN 3:1, AMP

He wants you in His family. It's where He made you to be. He wants *you*.

Not your stuff, not your money, not some big promise or vow that you're going to be morally upright. He doesn't even want the good things you've done or promise to do in the future, like tithing or serving.

He wants your heart. He wants you!

IDENTIFYING THE BARRIER

Remember, this isn't my idea—it's God's heart. And I'm eager that we never forget it. Hear the apostle Paul:

> May your roots go down deep into the soil of God's
> marvelous love; and may you be able to feel and
> understand, as all God's children should, how long,
> how wide, how deep, and how high his love really
> is; and to experience this love for yourselves.
>
> EPHESIANS 3:17–19, TLB

Have you experienced His love? Are you experiencing it still?

If your answer is no, it's time to get to the bottom of it—you've got to ask why. What good is it to *know* about God's love if you're not *experiencing* it?

Even if everything else in your life seems solid—you've got a good marriage, a decent income, a fine home, a good sense of sound doctrine—but your spiritual foundation is cracked, nonexistent, overlooked, broken, or self-contrived, then everything in your life will be unsteady. Nothing in your life, including your heart and eternity, will be sturdy. It will be like a house built on sand, and when the challenges of life beat against that house, it will come crashing down. No matter what it costs you, you must get this one clear.

My sister Pam understood that. That's why she did whatever it took to get my niece Leila into an environment where her experience of Jesus could move from her head to her heart. Leila is very much like her mother: left-brained, intelligent, and inquisitive, and she was beginning to ask insightful questions about God and spiritual matters. Pam knew what it was like to spend decades going to church, having a knowledge of

God but not necessarily experiencing God's love for herself. So she did the great work of seeing to it that Leila had a real opportunity to experience God's love before the decades began to add up. After Leila's week away at youth camp, where she decided to invite Christ into her heart and experience God's love for herself, it was obvious that the expense and effort was a pittance compared to the payoff. Leila's face said so much as her mother's prayers were answered.

> Ask yourself this question: What are the barriers preventing me from experiencing God's love?

I urge you to ask this question—one that only you and God can answer:

What are the barriers preventing me from experiencing God's love?

To help you identify your obstacles, here are some common barriers I've seen stand in many people's way:

- ☐ Unbelief
- ☐ Hurt
- ☐ Sin
- ☐ Fear
- ☐ Insecurity
- ☐ Control
- ☐ Spiritual pride
- ☐ _____

Do your best to identify what is in the way of you truly experiencing the love of God for yourself. Select one, write it down, say it out loud. "_____ is my barrier." In the end, it's just about being honest—an answer that's between you and God.

I remember the first time I taught this revolutionary truth in our church. It really stirred things up like nothing else. Longtime Questers took an honest look at the question I just asked you, and with humility, many acknowledged the gap. People like Slim and Sheridan, members of our drama team, decided that they'd lived long enough knowing *about* the love of God, but not experiencing His love for themselves, and gave their lives to Christ. Scores followed: Rachel, Lonnie, Amanda, Mike, Wendi, Brian, and countless others since! They were faithful churchgoers who'd been striving on the performance wheel too long, who'd finally said, "Enough's enough!" and welcomed Jesus' saving love into their hearts. The fruit, freedom, and overflow from their lives have been unmistakable. Love will do that to you.

Could it be that this is God's way of putting the car in park and coming around to the backseat to look into your heart of hearts, just to tell you, *I really love you. In fact, I made you to love you. So be honest with Me and with yourself. Isn't it time to live in My love?*

It's like your own version of Jeremiah 31, where God promises,

"I've never quit loving you and never will. Expect love, love, and more love! And so now I'll start over with you and build you up again." JEREMIAH 31:3, *THE MESSAGE*

Some of you hear those words and it's exactly what you need—to start over in the love of God. He's whispering possibility into your heart, getting behind your barriers just a little bit, lifting your heart with hope.

It's time to push play, my friend, and here are your traction steps:

1. Ask God to reveal your barriers to you.
2. Ask Him to demolish them.
3. Clear your calendar, make some real space, and engage in a conversation with your heavenly Father, asking Him to help you receive the love He's been dying for you to experience.

You were made to live in the love of God. For all the things in life that change, the love of God was always meant to be the constant in your heart: the strong foundation, the solid ground under your feet, the unshakable Truth that shapes and defines who you are. It's a love that threatens to rip open the skies and shout for the world to hear: *This is My son, My daughter, chosen and marked by My love, delight of My life!*

This is the unchanging reality about you, my friend:

God made you to love you.

GETTING TRACTION

REWIND

Your entire connection to God rises and falls on your ability to experience His love for you.

(↓) DOWNLOAD

This is my Son, whom I love; with him I am well pleased. MATTHEW 3:17, NIV

(▶) PUSH PLAY

Find thirty protected minutes and ask God to reveal your barriers to receiving His love. Ask Him to help you experience His love like you never have before.

Chapter 8

TIPPING POINT

LET'S JUST IMAGINE you ripped this page out of the book.

I said, "Imagine!" Hold up . . . stop! I didn't actually say to do it.

Now, *imagining* that you have this sheet of paper in hand, how many times do you think you could fold it in half before you would be unable to fold it anymore? It's approximately 1/100th of an inch thick—so even if you're not an arts and crafts person, what would your guess be?

Answer?

Seven. Seven folds are all you'll get.

Seems low, right?

I would agree with you, except my office has been littered

with paper trying to get to fold number eight —it can't be done. But don't take my word for it; go ahead—knock yourself out.

Alright, let's take this imagining a little further. What if you were able to fold this sheet of paper not just seven or eight times, but fifty? Any guesses on how tall our little sheet of paper would be? A few feet tall? Hundreds of feet tall? I've even heard someone guess a mile.

Answer: over ninety-three million miles tall!

This sheet of paper, if folded fifty times, would actually reach the sun!

It makes no sense, does it?

People smarter than me can give you an in-depth explanation, but it essentially boils down to one idea: exponential math. Adding a fold isn't just addition; it's compound multiplication, because you are folding every previous layer, exponentially growing the thickness of the paper.

Now, if I still have your attention (I know all my ADHD readers and most men have gone off to fold paper for the rest of the day, hoping to disprove this), don't worry. I'm done with the science lesson.

THE EXPONENTIAL EFFECT

Here's the point: When God begins to work in your life and you cooperate with Him, it has an exponential effect. Your one yes doesn't just add to the next yes and add to the next yes; the results are exponential! Your agreement, your collective yeses string together the same way the paper folds do. In the end, there is a mind-blowing effect, resulting in a supernatural impact on your life that defies common sense. Upon careful examination, the results might just elicit full-blown disbelief as common sense gets posterized and God's remarkable power takes you to heights you never would've thought possible.

When you string together a few yeses to God, an interesting thing begins to happen: you watch the water level in every area of your life begin to rise. First, *you* begin changing. Then you notice the change is spilling over into your marriage, your kids, your friends, and your school or workplace. Before long, you realize trans-

> When God begins to work in your life and you cooperate with Him, it has an exponential effect.

formation is inundating the deep places of your heart, dislodging fears, insecurities, pains, and strongholds. Your yeses overflow into all the challenging places of your life that have traditionally kicked your tail, and suddenly you realize that somehow God has begun to change *everything*!

That's what's at stake in every yes to God. Just think of Moses' successor, Joshua, as he led the Israelites across the Jordan River. Joshua 3:15-17 show that God led them to step into the flooded river before He did anything to see them through to the other side. As soon as they stepped into the water, God did for Joshua what He did for Moses; He parted the water before their very eyes. The entire nation of Israel crossed the Jordan on dry ground. As we observe Joshua's leadership in the years and decades to come, we see that he is forever changed by the miraculous events of Joshua 3. He saw God's power at work in his life and leadership that day in such an unexplainable way that a process was begun. He was bright enough to see the connection between God's power and his own willingness to agree and trust Him. Joshua did just as the Lord instructed, and the resultant impact changed his world forever. Certainly the changes affected his own life, but also every generation since.

Whatever the opportunity God has in front of you, realize this: it isn't small or insignificant. It's always part of the exponential math in the Transformation Adventure for your life.

THE QUICK FIX

We tend to think that if God wants to change our lives, He ought to start and finish it right now. His dramatic renovations should all be completed instantly.

My son Carson has always been quite a baller. From the time he was able to stand on his own two feet, he's loved playing ball with his big brother, Corey, shooting hoops out in the cul-de-sac, playing with every neighbor and friend who'd give him five minutes.

While he loved playing around the house, nothing compared to the day when he was finally old enough to play in an official basketball league! Now he would be coached and trained to play with the best of them. A dream come true.

As his first game approached, Carsi's excitement couldn't

be contained. He was pump-faking, jive dunking—running up and down the hallway in the house getting ready for the big game. I think he thought he was Wildcat great John Wall or something.

He was about to leave for his first game when he stopped dead in his tracks, looked at his mom with a very concerned expression on his face, and said, "Oh, no. I forgot to ask Coach if you're allowed to dunk in this league."

Two practices down, nowhere near tall enough to ride the thrill rides at Sea World, and he thinks he ought to be able to make a highlight reel receiving alley-oops from Dwyane Wade like LeBron.

Have you ever felt that way? Ever given God access to something in your heart or life, and then expected Him to immediately accomplish all that needed to be done? Maybe it's been sharing your faith or learning to trust Him with your finances, or maybe it's just been as simple as actually going to church and making it feel like home. We *finally* get our courage up to deal with a major area, and we're thinking the least God could do is hit us with His version of *Extreme Home Makeover* and then . . . move that bus! *Bam!* Transformation accomplished. When we get honest with God, our prayers sound a lot like this: "If You're offering real change, God, I'll take it *now*."

I was recently doing some reading about plastic surgeries, the quintessential "now" fix to whatever physical transformation we want to see in our lives. I ran across an interesting book written in 1936 entitled, *New Faces, New Futures* by Maxwell

Maltz, a doctor who chronicled his experiences of helping those who sought transformation through plastic surgery.

His work dealt primarily with women, specifically those who came in believing that if they could just get this quick fix, they would be happy. Hundreds of transformed faces, noses, eyes, arms, and other body parts later, Dr. Maltz's work was just beginning. Subsequent to people's surgeries, he began a follow-up process that lasted for several years, compiling his findings and looking for trends. His conclusions were quite clear: people who came in looking for a fresh start by fixing something on the outside were *just* as dissatisfied, insecure, and discouraged on the inside after surgery as they had been before.

> Superficial alterations do not accomplish supernatural transformations.

Is plastic surgery not your thing? I've studied the lives of lottery winners as well. If anything could accomplish quick, lasting transformation, then a sudden infusion of millions of dollars should, right? The surprising reality is that most of those people, when all was said and done, wished they hadn't won. Read the interviews with former lottery winners for yourself. The majority of them take a sharp turn downward. They end up lonely and disappointed; their lives become confused and complicated. Sadly, some have even taken their lives after dealing with the resultant damage to their hearts and minds. You'd be shocked at the number of people who say, "I wish I'd never won in the first place."

Do you know why plastic surgeries and winning lottery

tickets don't actually solve anything? Because *superficial alter-ations do not accomplish supernatural transformations.* You can engineer a brand-new face or become a multimillionaire over-night, but inside, you are still you. It's the same old you—with the same old heart, carrying around all your struggles, strained relationships, troubling proclivities, messed-up his-tory, and tainted thought patterns. Those external superficial alterations cannot make the adjustments that an all-powerful God can on the inside.

If transformation were just about instant results, then nothing would actually change for the long haul. Why? Because we, as human beings, need the benefit of process. We need the benefit of developments that occur over time.

WORTH THE WAIT

Ladies, what if I was to tell you that all the diamonds in your possession—every family heirloom, your engagement ring, everything—were less than perfect? I don't just mean some inward defect that a jeweler would notice. I mean, what if you found out right now that your jewels were actually all cubic zirconia?

After you send the men in your lives to the nearest ER to get stitched up, I'd like you to answer this question: why would it matter? Your jewelry looks and feels the same as it did before. Nobody will be able to tell the difference except a jeweler or someone with a trained eye. No one knows. It looks and feels the same.

Before you completely write me off, let me clarify: of course it matters! There has been a fraud somewhere along the line. You have a counterfeit, a fake. Somehow, someone misled you, and you don't have the priceless gem you thought you had. You have something far less valuable.

Now, men, before you start dreaming up ways to scrimp on diamonds by investing in CZ, here's the technical explanation behind why diamonds are worth investing in. In the right setting, you can make cubic zirconia in just a few days. It's not a difficult process. They're pretty, they're cheap, and they're easy to make. It makes sense: that which is cheap is really easy to make.

Diamonds, on the other hand, take an extremely long time to form. It requires enormous amounts of pressure, heat, and time to forge a natural diamond. What begins as something quite unimpressive becomes mesmerizingly gorgeous. The long process produces a remarkable gem, carrying with it two consistent but rare qualities: extreme strength and the ability to disperse light.

Isn't that the perfect picture of what God does in us during this Transformation Adventure of life? Day after day, through the pressures of life and the heat of trials, He is making you into something beautiful, endowed with extreme strength and the ability to disperse His light. Wouldn't it be great to be someone who doesn't break easily, even in the extreme heat of life circumstances? What about being someone who disperses the light of Christ, even in the darkest places?

This is what God is up to on your Transformation Adventure. He knows how lasting growth and deep change occur. If we will commit to a lifestyle of daily yeses—agreeing and cooperating with Him as He leads us—then He will do the transforming work.

The exponential power unlocked by your instant yeses to God will take your breath away, not because you're the one saying them, but because of whom you are saying them to!

Some yeses are basic; some are exhilarating. God rarely gives you 201-, 301-, or 401-level opportunities to grapple with until you've learned to say the simpler 101-level yeses. If you've ever looked at the lives of people around you and thought to yourself, *Why has God never asked me to do big things?* then I would ask you this: what have you done with His requests in the small things?

The exponential power of saying yes to God always begins with small things. One yes leads to the next few; the next few lead to the next dozen; the next dozen lead to a whole new level of saying yes. It becomes so automatic for you to live out 101-level yeses, that in time, you are given the opportunity to become fluent at the 201 level.

> The exponential power of saying yes to God always begins with small things.

You begin to realize that you are actually changing from the inside out. You're loving people you didn't care about in the past. You're serving without thinking of how you are being cared for. You're giving away your treasures, becoming a generous person with your resources and enjoying it. Eventually you reflect on where you are now—as compared to where you started—and you think to yourself, *This is nuts!*

You may not know exactly how it all happened—it may have been almost imperceptible to you as it occurred—but the change is undeniable. The Holy Spirit does His work as you agree, and then one day as you look in the mirror, it dawns on you: "I have become more like Jesus and less like the person I was without Him!" Through God's transforming power and your willing spirit, you find that you are largely unrecognizable from who you used to be. You have reached a tipping point in your journey. You are actually becoming Christlike.

> One day as you look in the mirror, it dawns on you: "I have become more like Jesus and less like the person I was without Him!"

THE GREAT MIRACLE AND THE GREAT LIE

When I had my first son, it wasn't immediately clear who Corey was going to look like. Some people thought me, others thought my wife, Jacki, but it was tough to tell. However, as he grew up, it became clearer and clearer: this boy could almost be my clone. He looks like me, sounds like me, walks like me, laughs like me, and when you put our pictures from the same ages side by side, the resemblance is uncanny.

But just because Corey looks like me on the outside, that doesn't mean we're going to resemble one another on the inside. That's based on *his* yeses and nos, *his* choices, *his* everyday responses to God.

When you gave your life to Christ through a sincere conversation with God, asking for His forgiveness for your sins, do you realize what happened? He instantly erased the record of sins and charges against you (see Colossians 2:13-14). He forgave *all* your sins—past, present, and future. That's why His grace is so astonishing.

However, He did not instantly give you Christlike character. You may remember this earlier statement from chapter 2: *The redemption of your soul takes only a moment; the reclamation of your character takes a lifetime.*

The minute you prayed and gave your life to Christ, the greatest miracle that will ever take place in your life occurred: you were washed clean, completely forgiven—you were born again into the family of God! But here's the thing I believe so many of us miss: while it is the Great Miracle, it is not the whole miracle.

I'll never forget May 24, 1991. After years of dating, months of planning, and a few final harrowing days, I was going to marry the girl of my dreams. As the music swelled and Jacki rounded the corner of the back of the church she'd grown up in, I suddenly found myself breathless. I nearly fell apart. She was beautiful, gorgeous, even more than usual. At last she was about to become my bride. It was the culmination of a beautiful process of falling in love, learning to do life together, and listening to Jesus. Now the big moment was here: our wedding day! While this certainly was a day among days, it wasn't the finish line; it was a starting gate. The beauty, the change, the joy, the challenge, the grand adventure was just beginning.

Similarly, when you experienced the miracle of new life in Christ, it was never meant to conclude after one day! The Great Miracle is meant to be a continuing reality in your life, but it won't be if you fall for the Great Lie.

The Great Lie is that the great miracle of conversion is the whole miracle of God.

So many people give their lives to Jesus and then over time, as the difficult work of transformation continues, they fall prey to the Great Lie. The diamond-forming process in their own hearts has been slow to come, so they begin to think that maybe their best moments with God are behind them. They resign themselves to the idea that mediocre growth is the best they can expect and that Jesus has removed their names from the "To Be Used Greatly by God" list.

> The Great Lie is that the great miracle of conversion is the whole miracle of God.

The insidious power of the Great Lie isn't that it denies the miracle of conversion. In fact, it highlights and celebrates it. But it *leaves it in the past*. The Great Lie says, "The work of God is over in your life; it's complete. Don't expect too much, and quit getting your hopes up." If you've had those thoughts, then I've got tough news for you—you've believed the Lie.

But all heaven is in adamant disagreement—and you can be too! God is not done. You can quit listening to the Great Lie and the great liar telling you, "You're never going to change, grow, or move beyond your present circumstances." You don't have to give that voice one more moment of your attention. Instead, listen to the Spirit of Truth:

The Spirit of God, who raised Jesus from the dead, lives in you. And just as God raised Christ Jesus from the dead, he will give life to your mortal bodies by the same Spirit living within you.   ROMANS 8:11

It's in Christ that we find out who we are and what we are living for. Long before we first heard of Christ and got our hopes up, he had his eye on us, had designs on us for glorious living, part of the overall purpose he is working out in everything and everyone.   EPHESIANS 1:11–12, THE MESSAGE

Forget the former things; do not dwell on the past. See, I am doing a new thing! Now it springs up; do you not perceive it?   ISAIAH 43:18–19, NIV

The Holy Spirit who brought Jesus back from the dead is doing amazing work in you, my friend. He is transforming you, changing you, filling you with the mind of God, the heart of Jesus, and the character of Christ. Jesus is alive and at work in your life—the Great Miracle continues!

AN OFFERING

Why does it matter so much that we get our hearts and minds around that reality?

First, it means that you can stop getting discouraged if change is slow to come. Just like diamond formation, this doesn't happen overnight. Resist the urge to bail. Don't stop—you're on the right track. The answer isn't trying harder; it's trusting harder. Leave the speed of the journey to God; you just keep cooperating.

> If change is slow to come, the answer isn't trying harder—it's trusting harder. Leave the speed of the journey to God.

Second, you can identify the most change-resistant areas in your life and submit them to God today. What are the top three areas that have your number? Can you name them? Are they related to money, sex, anger, porn, pride, addiction, unforgiveness, insecurity, isolation? The Great Miracle means that God is more committed than you are to transforming these areas in your life. You can join Him.

Seem too simple?

For over two thousand years, the Bible has been laying out the recipe for how this works. It's been right under our noses the whole time. Listen to what the apostle Paul writes in Romans 12:

> So here's what I want you to do, God helping you:
> Take your everyday, ordinary life—your sleeping,
> eating, going-to-work, and walking-around life—and
> place it before God as an offering. Embracing what
> God does for you is the best thing you can do for him.
> Don't become so well-adjusted to your culture that
> you fit into it without even thinking. Instead, fix your
> attention on God. You'll be changed from the inside

out. Readily recognize what he wants from you, and quickly respond to it. Unlike the culture around you, always dragging you down to its level of immaturity, God brings the best out of you, develops well-formed maturity in you.   ROMANS 12:1-2, *THE MESSAGE*

God's Word couldn't be clearer.

When you're filled with His Spirit, you have access to a power you can't manufacture on your own—and it's your yes that releases Him to do what you cannot. I don't care how many episodes of *Dr. Phil* you watch or how many Tony Robbins conferences you attend; lasting transformation won't happen apart from God. Superficial alterations do not accomplish supernatural transformations.

DOUG: TIPPING-POINT EVIDENCE

Curveball.

Ever wonder how Jesus was ready to die? How was He ready to say yes to the cross?

In one respect, I believe it was surprisingly simple: three decades of never saying a no to His Father. Or, for our purposes, *three decades of yeses to God.* For thirty years, Jesus just said one yes after another. His heart was in continual agreement: "Yes, Dad, I will go. Yes, I will speak. Yes, Father, I will pray. Yes, I will share Your heart with them. Yes, Dad. Yes, yes, yes."

The only reason that heaven is available to any of us is because Jesus said His yeses.

What would it mean to offer Him your cooperation every single day?

I remember when my friend Doug decided to do that. A veteran of the police department for a dozen years, he had given his life to Christ a few years earlier. I will never forget the moment when the Great Miracle and Doug collided. Christ broke through decades of skepticism, pain, and hardness of heart, and Doug gave his life to Jesus! Since then, years had passed, and while he wasn't the same old Doug anymore, he wasn't the completely new Doug either.

And then, one January, something tipped in him.

He'd heard countless stories of people who were being transformed by Jesus. Suddenly the thought occurred to him: *What if I just said yes?* Doug, the practical thinker that he is, set a goal for himself. *What if for the next year, I just said yes to God—no matter what, no matter when, no matter where?*

> What would it mean to offer Him your cooperation every single day?

So he did. Doug gave a "yes in advance" to whatever God had for him.

The best way to describe him a year later?

Unrecognizable.

Something shifted in Doug through his resolute agreement. A simple yes, followed by another yes, began yielding compound interest in his life. Old patterns began breaking away, and his heart became soft to God. The cynic in him died, and a newly transformed Doug began to take his place. Everyone around him saw the change—it was impossible to miss.

So what if you just decided to start saying yes?

I've seen it more times than I can count. Just like Doug, you'll start to see the math of your yeses add up. Not by addition—by exponential multiplication.

God can change you from the inside out. Picture yourself changing from insecure to confident, selfish to servant, skeptical to trusting, weak to strong—from cubic zirconia to diamond. When you reject the Great Lie, "positive contamination" is released through your active agreement. You begin to see the water level rising in the lives of the people around you. God's power and your yeses have begun to shape you into a diamond, strong and radiant for Christ.

PAR: A CONCRETE WAY TO SAY YES

If you're ready to begin saying yes, I want to share with you a simple acrostic that I've come back to again and again. For over a decade, I've watched this simple tool help others as they've practiced saying yes to the work and will of God in their lives.

Position Yourself Well

We each have to take the responsibility to put ourselves near the people and places that catalyze transformation. Who will encourage and challenge you to go in the direction that God wants you to go? Much of the time our growth gets stalled out, not because God's Spirit isn't able, but because we've positioned ourselves poorly.

There are places you need to start getting to, and there are places you need to stop going to. Where do you need to be to position yourself well to engage in the work of transformation?

> We each have to take the responsibility to put ourselves near the people and places that catalyze transformation.

Is it attending weekend church services, stepping into Christian counseling, or attending an AA meeting or some other form of life-changing community where you can be authentic in your pursuit of Jesus? Or perhaps you need to stop going some places: the cubicle of the coworker who's been so easy to flirt with, the bar on the way home from work, a certain site on the Internet, or maybe the presence of that person who is impacting you so negatively.

Only you can position yourself well. Do what you need to do. Today!

Advance Decision-Making

This is simply deciding what things you will and won't do—before the heat gets turned up. If we wait to make decisions until we're face-to-face with temptation, then we're left at the whim of our weaknesses. We may not always choose perfectly, but choosing in advance improves the odds.

When you decide who you're going to be and how you're going to act before you find yourself in the heat of the moment, you begin to discover that you're proactively sidestepping the same old battles. Your trajectory begins to steer away from the things that have typically run all over

PETE HISE

you. But it begins when we make our choice *now*: "I'm not going to wait until I'm in the backseat of a car, or on that website, or at the casino, or with my friends, to think 'Should I do this or should I not?' I am deciding *now*."

Advance decision-making also works in the other direction. What if you decided in advance to become a tither, to be baptized, to take a step closer to God, to share your faith with your neighbors, or to invite your friend to church this weekend? Let's not weigh out those positive growth opportunities in the moment; let's push play now on the decisions we need to make.

> We may not always choose perfectly, but choosing in advance improves the odds.

Resolve to Live a Self-Examined Life

We all have blind spots. None of us see the entirety of our lives with 20/20 clarity. God wants us operating in the truth, but we need to be diligent if we're going to take stock of how we're really doing. Life is busy. Even in our desire to be shaped into the people Christ designed us to be, it's all too easy to lose track and neglect the question, "So how am I doing—really?" When is the last time you conducted an internal inventory?

What steps can you take to make sure that you're regularly "looking into the mirror" to see how you're doing in your own transformation? Perhaps it's carving out fifteen to twenty minutes a day specifically to meet with God— to read His Word and invite Him to shine His light on

When is the last time you conducted an internal inventory?

your progress. Or maybe you need to find a small group of people who will help you honestly assess how you're doing. Ask trustworthy people for feedback. We all have blind spots, but when you're living a self-examined life, you may find that the tools and the motivation to help you begin tipping in the direction God has in mind.

IT'S TIME

Don't you think it's time you begin seeing the ratio in your life shift? It really is possible. One day you can look in the mirror and realize that, through God's power and your cooperation, you are actually beginning to resemble Jesus, who gave His life on the cross for you.

It happened in Doug's life. It's been seven years since he started saying one yes after another. He's now on the board of directors, doing all he can to see that our church does all it can to help people step wholeheartedly into their Transformation Adventure. Doug can hardly believe who he is these days . . . and neither can I. He is looking more and more like Jesus, and so can you. What if you followed in Doug's footsteps and gave God one full year of unqualified yeses? You will not be disappointed with the changes God effects in your heart. It's time to let the exponential power of God loose in your life—you may be closer to the tipping point than you think.

GETTING TRACTION

REWIND

Superficial alterations do not accomplish supernatural transformations.

DOWNLOAD

So here's what I want you to do, God helping you: Take your everyday, ordinary life—your sleeping, eating, going-to-work, and walking-around life—and place it before God as an offering. Embracing what God does for you is the best thing you can do for him. Don't become so well-adjusted to your culture that you fit into it without even thinking. Instead, fix your attention on God. You'll be changed from the inside out. Readily recognize what he wants from you, and quickly respond to it. Unlike the culture around you, always dragging you down to its level of immaturity, God brings the best out of you, develops well-formed maturity in you. ROMANS 12:1-2, THE MESSAGE

PUSH PLAY

PAR: A Concrete Way to Say Yes
Position Yourself Well
Advance Decision-Making
Resolve to Live a Self-Examined Life

Chapter 9

OVERTHROWN

WHAT IF YOU WERE worth 1.1 billion dollars?

What if you owned several houses and your spouse was a supermodel? Suppose every time you walked into a room, everyone would turn just to look at the one on your arm. You'd glance back with a smug look that said, "Yeah, she's with me." They'd look at you, look at your spouse, then look back at you. Jealousy would strike hard. (My wife tells me she goes through this *all* the time. Must be difficult for her.)

What if you were commonly regarded as one of the greatest athletes of your generation, or perhaps of all time? What if you were ranked number one in the world for three straight years, with people constantly saying, "There will never be another!" and Oprah and President Obama placed just below you on the "Most Recognized Celebrity" list?

In case you're not tracking, I'm not talking about you—unless your name is Tiger Woods.

In 2009, Tiger had it all—everything I've just listed and more. None of us can hope to accomplish and rise to the level that Tiger had achieved. In every sense of the word, he was a phenom. And he was happy.

Or was he?

In November 2009, there was a car accident involving Tiger Woods that occurred just outside his home. At first, it seemed like Tiger was fine, despite the damages. But it turned out that the collision was symptomatic of deeper damage that was far worse than anyone knew at the time.

Before long the entire world began to learn the real story.

Soon, every news outlet was broadcasting the secret life of Tiger Woods: he was having an affair with another woman. And sadly, not *just* one woman—eleven women identified themselves as Tiger's mistresses. It didn't compute. He was married to a supermodel! He was at the top of his game, he was raking in millions, his fame was planet-wide—so why the affairs?

Tiger Woods wasn't satisfied—not with a billion dollars, mansions, yachts, around-the-clock applause, and a supermodel wife. He wanted more . . . lots more. What Tiger thought would satiate his hunger was all of this—*and* eleven affairs on the side. Lust had become a power-hungry idol in his life, and even the legendary Tiger Woods proved to be no match for it.

Here's the bottom line: I'm not pointing a condemning

finger at Tiger. I've prayed lots of times that he would come to know Jesus personally and discover the only love that will ever truly fill him up. But Tiger, in this case, is no exception to the rule. The phenom and the common people like you and me are the same. I've seen this same mind-set in all of us—"I have everything, yet I still need _____." I've seen it in people of all walks of life: pastors, authors, doctors, cops, actors, mechanics . . . take your pick. Tiger's exposure made us stand up and take notice, but it's an ancient reality that has dogged people of every generation: "If only I had *this*, then I'd be happy."

A NEW DEFINITION

The "Tiger Principle" has proved to be so tempting to the human race that it got targeted in the first of ten very famous commandments. It's as if God knew how much of a stumbling block this could be, so He gave us a clear path so we'd know what it truly meant to follow Him in such tricky territory. Exodus says,

> You must not have any other god but me. You must not make for yourself an idol of any kind or an image of anything in the heavens or on the earth or in the sea. You must not bow down to them or worship them, for I, the LORD your God, am a jealous God who will not tolerate your affection for any other gods. EXODUS 20:3-5

I know what you're thinking: Is this guy really going to start talking about *idolatry*? I get that. A quick look around your home, and it probably wouldn't yield any Zeus statues, totem poles, or golden calves. We tend to think that idolatry was the scourge of a bygone era, or at least that it's disappeared into the far reaches of third-world countries. So would it shock you to know that I suspect that most of us have idols in our lives right now? I'm willing to bet that

Anything other than God that vies for our devotion may well be an idol.

some of us have even made them with our own hands and have set up a place of worship for them in our own lives.

God defines reality for us just as He did for ancient Israel: "If you don't want to be My people, that's your call. But if you want to be My children, here's how it works: put Me first in your heart . . . over everything else." Just like the Hebrews in Exodus, we aren't expected to do this perfectly without failing, but the expectation is clear: God is all you need to make you happy. Anything else that attempts to assume His throne in your heart is a counterfeit and an idol.

Seem overboard? Too old-school for you? Perhaps a definition of idolatry would help us:

Idolatry: to have undue affection for and be excessively devoted to something, such that it competes with your worship of and dependence on God.

Did you catch that? Anything other than God that vies for our devotion may well be an idol. It thins our resolve, transforming us from those who say, "I need only God," into people who mean, "I need God . . . and all this other stuff."

FEELING DERAILED?

Life on the Transformation Adventure is awesome.

Once you've pushed play and you're actually going for it, you start to feel the wind at your back like you're really growing and moving in the right direction. But all too often another scenario begins to occur. A month or two down the road, something happens. All of a sudden there's a tug backward. You feel a difference in your core.

What's this weight on my shoulder? I was feeling so good; why do I now find myself struggling so badly? You feel a little like you're being pulled in the opposite direction. In the middle of fantastic progress, you find yourself increasingly derailed from the path you were on, as if you're the victim of a spiritual coup being staged from the inside out. It feels like you're being overthrown. Like something that feels just beyond your immediate control is steering you almost, but not exactly, against your wishes.

It happened to a good friend of mine who experienced a derailment before my eyes. She had volunteered with joy and fulfillment, was so grateful to God for rescuing her, and was stepping into the plans Jesus had for her. Until, that is, she came face-to-face with something that she'd allowed to stay in the corner of her heart—a small idol was revealed. You see, my friend was mostly content in her life with Christ, but she had a secret fear that she would end up alone. She had trouble trusting God with her relational world . . . so she didn't. Even if it meant finding her own solution, she was not going to be lonely. And that brought on a world of hurt.

Her situation was manageable for a time, until one day a man came along who chose and pursued her. Rather than trusting God for His timing and provision, she lunged at what she was desperate to possess—a relationship. She finally got what she wanted. It didn't take long until the passion for serving God was tempered by doing whatever it took to keep this guy. The dreams of God were discarded in the wake of her decision to manufacture her own. She eventually stepped out of serving (despite loving it) and faded from impact. God's dreams became just a yawning emptiness inside her. In the years since this unanticipated derailment, I have reflected with her over her choices and the potential that has been diverted. We know from Genesis 50:20 that what the enemy intended for harm, God will use for His good purposes. But for now, "what if?" is a painful question for her.

The bad news is that this isn't an uncommon experience. Yet that doesn't make it any less lethal. People allow idols to go unchecked in the corners of their hearts, and when the opportunity arises, they often go chasing after them, while the dreams of God for their lives are squandered.

Proverbs 16:25 gets right to the point:

There is a way that seems right to a man, but in the
end it leads to death. (NIV)

The good news is that it doesn't have to go this way; it
is not an inevitable experience for every follower of Christ.

You don't have to be overthrown; you don't have to be
complicit. You are not destined to play the
victim. You may feel powerless, but that's
not reality. Call to mind the revolutionary
truth from Romans 8:11 that the Spirit
of God resides inside every true child of
God. The same Spirit who took Jesus'
dead body and raised it to life is alive and
active in *you*!

> The Spirit of God resides inside every true child of God. The same Spirit who took Jesus' dead body and raised it to life is alive and active in *you*!

You may say, "But you don't know the
challenges I face. . . ." You're right. I don't.
But God does, and He has made prepa-
rations to handle them. In case you are
tempted to think that your problems are a little too much
for the Holy Spirit, keep this in mind: death wasn't too big a
challenge for Him. Remember, Jesus was dead and lifeless in
the grave. And then the Holy Spirit interrupted, "Um, I'm
not done here. I'm just getting started! Count down the days:
3, 2, 1. When Sunday arrives, you'll see this man alive, and
you'll never need to doubt My power again!"

What if we decide to let the Holy Spirit do His work in
us? Rather than just believing that God is able to address the
needs of the world, suppose we begin to believe that He is

able to help *us* face our struggles and challenges, to overthrow the idols that are vying for our worship.

JONNY: BREAKING FREE

I've known my friend Jonny since he was a kid. His parents did ministry with me for years, and it became clear pretty early on that he was a gifted, creative artist burgeoning with the promise of how God might use his life. When the day came that Jonny realized he was relying on his good behavior and the heritage of his parents for his salvation, he humbled himself and chose to enter into a relationship with Christ *for himself*. It was a day of great celebration! Jonny's real life was just beginning.

As he took his first steps in following Christ, we saw the gifts and talents that God had planted in Jonny start to come to life. But as he served and invested in the creative process, a gap began to emerge. Jonny had lots of opinions about how things should go, and with those thoughts came lots of judgments about how they *shouldn't*. His grateful heart of worship started to be contaminated by a desire to see *his* creative ideas chosen, *his* songs and designs honored and celebrated, things going *his* way. This young, promising artist found himself honoring Jesus with his words while being consumed with honoring himself at the same time—an irreconcilable combination. He hated the conflict within his heart. The battle within became consuming; he would take two steps forward, then three steps back. Something had to give.

In the middle of that conflict, Jesus brought help through an unlikely circumstance. Jonny came to me to confess an area of sin in his life. Next he took steps of repentance and humility, and he received forgiveness and grace in a deep way. He let love do its healing work in his heart. So much so that his worship began to be affected by the reality of his rescue; his gratitude flowed from a place of profound forgiveness. And while his struggle with critical thoughts and self-consumption wasn't over, soon those things were no longer at the forefront of his mind. Gratitude has a way of making idols fade—especially the idol of self. The amazing grace of God will do that in a person.

These days, I'd have to say that Jonny is one of the most grateful people I know. A heart that was full of self-worship is now overwhelmed by the fact that Jesus chose *him*. In the process of thanking Jesus with his life, Jonny forgets to advance himself; when that happens, true worship begins to flow. Jesus has done a new thing in Jonny's heart. Jonny let the idol of self fall as he's fallen more and more in love with the Rescuer of his heart. So much so that a couple of years ago, I asked Jonny to come on staff and honor Jesus with the best hours of his day. He is truly a trophy of God's healing, transforming grace.

There's nothing quite like experiencing real transformation, the thrill of actual, personal change. It catches you by surprise.

You see an attractive woman, and instead of thinking the kind of thoughts you've had for twenty years, you begin to see her the way Jesus does.

Your idea of a way to make some quick money is interrupted midstream by the thought of who may get hurt by your plan.

When the credit goes to someone else, rather than asking "what about me?" you find yourself cheering them on.

Rather than yelling in the midst of a family crisis, you hear yourself suddenly suggest, "Can we pray about this?" I can imagine the response: "Did Dad just say we should pray? Has he been drinking?"

> Most things in life can be stolen, but not what Christ does on the inside.

Transformation feels phenomenal, like the Cowboys blowing out the Redskins at FedEx Field. It's just as good as it gets. It's something no one else can take away from you. Most things in life can be stolen, but not what Christ does on the inside. That's the kind of transformation that *lasts*. When God starts to change your heart and you agree, nothing feels better than that.

"JESUS" OR "JESUS AND . . ."

So can I tell you something tough to hear?

Your progress is not going to last if you don't deal with the idolatry in your life.

You will feel the tug of the rope. You will get tangled and tripped up fast by idolatry. Suddenly, you're three steps back instead of the two forward you felt so good about. Idolatry—if not dealt with—will land you right back at the starting line.

Do you know the feeling?

It happens when you give an idol power in your life. The Scriptures are clear: the One True God won't have it. He wants all of you—not a fraction (see Joshua 24:14-15).

When we give our lives to Christ, what we tell Him is much like what a bride and groom say to each other at the altar: "for better, for worse . . . in sickness and in health . . . we'll do this together." The level of singular devotion is the same in a relationship with Jesus. "My heart, my worship, my devotion is Yours, Lord. I commit to and enter into this exclusive relationship—a relationship that supersedes the one I have with my spouse, my kids, my career, and my calling."

When I married my wife, Jacki, I committed myself to *her*. I didn't say "I do" and actually mean I would also keep a few other wives on the down-low in other places so no one else would find out. I committed to her and her alone—an exclusive relationship.

> The Scriptures are clear: the One True God wants all of you—not a fraction.

If you've given your life to Jesus, that's what you said. And by saying that, you said no to all other suitors (read: *idols*). To our credit, when it's put like that, many of us think, *I would never be unfaithful to Jesus. He died for me. I love Him. I belong to Him, therefore I will be true.*

And then the storm comes.

Unexpected difficulty sets in, and it begins to expose something buried in your heart.

What if there is no spouse to come? Are you okay with just you and Jesus?

What if there are no children?

What if your health doesn't improve?

What if "they" never apologize for the hurt they caused you?

What if there is no recognition and no applause for your efforts?

What if the money doesn't pour in?

What if the big dreams and plans you've been asking God to bless never come to pass?

Can you be satisfied—in light of all life's disappointments—with Jesus alone? To have Him present with you every step of your journey? I didn't say that makes you want to throw a party all the time. In fact, the Bible tells us to cry when it's right to cry, and to be sad when it makes sense to be sad. It also says that God is near to the brokenhearted, but He may not always prevent the things that cause brokenheartedness. Unfortunately, people sin all the time, and the bad choices that are made have profound implications. But all the while,

> **Can you be satisfied with Jesus alone?**

Jesus says, "I'm faithful and true. I'll walk with you through the storms, never leaving you to face your perils alone."

Each of us must answer this life-pivoting question with all the clarity and honesty we're able to muster: What will ultimately reside at the center of my life, defining my sense of satisfaction and meaning? Will I need only Jesus or "Jesus *and* _____ (you fill in the blank)"? You know what I mean: Underneath it all, we say, "I'll be fine! As long as I have Jesus *and* comfort!" Or Jesus *and* approval. Or Jesus *and* security. Or Jesus *and* riches . . . image . . . love . . . children. You can make your own list, because it's your life and you get to choose.

> *Only you can choose to be true to the One who is always true to you.*

Jesus tells us in Matthew 6:24 that if you decide to be devoted to two gods, you will live a divided life, and it will be unstable on every level. However, if you choose to serve God alone, you will emerge strong and steadfast. *Only you* can choose to be true to the One who is always true to you.

Jesus at the center, or Jesus *and* . . . ?

It's your decision.

THE CALL TO A SINGULAR HEART

One of my favorite people in the Bible is Joshua.

His story is well known. Starting off as Moses' assistant, he got a front-row seat to the astonishing things that Oscar Award–winning movies have been made about. Later, when it was time for Moses to be done, Joshua was commissioned as the new leader of Israel. He took the baton from the heavyweight, Moses, and received a special outpouring of God's Spirit. He had his own parting of the water as the people of Israel crossed the Jordan River into the Promised Land. The next decades of his life were filled with victory after victory as he led his people into battle after battle to lay claim to the

Promised Land. His whole life, from front to back, is a story of extraordinary faithfulness to God. I highly encourage you to read it for yourself in the Old Testament book that bears his name.

While Joshua was a favorite hero of mine from the moment I saw his character in *The Ten Commandments*, I remember when the heart of Joshua became clear to me. After having been a Christian for three or four months, I visited the home of my friend Peggy, whose entire family were Christ-followers. As I stood at their front door and knocked, I noticed a small metal cross affixed to their door with these words written on it:

> Choose for yourselves this day whom you will
> serve. . . . As for me and my household, we will
> serve the Lord.

Cool. This tiny door decoration reflected how I wanted to live my entire life—faithful to God. I was stunned when I looked more closely and realized that the guy who said this was my man, Josh.

The famous quote comes from Joshua 24, the final chapter of his book and the last scene of his life. The people of Israel are gathered at Shechem, including the leaders, military officers, priests, and as many Israelites as he could muster. His intention was to levy a challenge with his last breath to the people he had led for decades: "Choose this day whom you will serve." It went stunningly well! Their response?

"We would never abandon the Lord and serve other gods" (Joshua 24:16).

But Joshua didn't buy it.

He had seen firsthand how people often declared their devotion to the Lord but didn't mean it. He knew the damage of a divided heart. I can imagine him saying, "You sound convincing, but in your heart there are reservations."

Have you had places like that, where you've been solid in your declaration but halfhearted in your devotion?

Joshua wasn't interested in popularity; he wasn't running for office. He was serving God with a singular heart. So he lovingly but sternly warned the people with the consequences of their wandering devotion. But once again, their response was emphatic: "No, we will serve the Lord!" (Joshua 24:21).

> Have you been solid in your declaration but halfhearted in your devotion?

And then Joshua utters this odd sentence: "You are a witness to your own decision" (verse 22).

"Yes, we are witnesses to what we've said," they agree.

You get the impression that Joshua takes a deep breath. "I've done all I can do. Moses, my mentor, led you. I have led you for year upon year upon year. And now you swear here at Shechem, a holy place, that you'll serve God and God alone, not the other gods."

Then the old warrior looks them in the eye and says, "All right then, destroy the idols among you, and turn your hearts to the Lord" (Joshua 24:23). The famous assistant-turned-biblical-hero urges them with his final charge: "Overthrow and destroy the idols you've taken up among you and be finished. If you're serious about this, eliminate any other option. If you're going to serve God, do it with everything."

Like the people of Israel, we also make similar claims and mean them in divided ways. Our idols may look different from theirs, but they are just as powerful. They impact our lives profoundly. Joshua's warning still applies: if you're serious about making God first in your life, then destroy all other suitors.

Some of us, without ever clearly stating it, are hanging our hearts, hopes, and plans on a fantasy life we are idolizing. We act like we can manage and compartmentalize two separate worlds—one with marriage, kids, bills, responsibilities, etc.; the other with secret lusts, indulgences, relationships, and pursuits. But Joshua, God's man, shouts to us across the ages, "Are you going to live in the real world or a fantasy world? If you're going to serve God, then destroy, burn, overthrow the other option entirely." If it's God you're going to serve, make it God.

What will be first in your life? Will it be the God who would rather die than live without you, or will it be the things you cling to, the stuff of the fantasy life you are playing out in your mind? Will you offer Him only half your heart or all of it? Will you hang your hopes on Him or on the life you fantasize about?

PARTIAL OBEDIENCE

One of the sins that the people of God were often held responsible for in the Old Testament is something I call *par-*

tial obedience. Here's what it looked like: the people of God would face an enemy with clear instructions from the Lord. "I'll go with you into battle. I'll give you this land. We will be victorious. Once that happens, I want you to destroy everything. Not just the enemy—I want you to destroy it all. Crops, furniture, homes, places of worship, idols, sacred books, silver and gold—I want it all gone."

But in a heartbreaking story repeated again and again throughout the Old Testament, the people obey God—mostly. They destroy *mostly* everything, sometimes keeping riches of silver and gold, or perhaps the enemy's king to pridefully parade around. Their response when the truth comes out? "We did everything you said . . . except maybe this one thing." And to obey God mostly is tantamount to disobedience.

So why did God call for such a dramatic response in the first place?

Parents, how many times have your kids inadvertently asked for something harmful? They thought it would be cool, fun, or exciting, but you knew better. So you protected them—even against their will. A father's love will do that sometimes.

God knew the power of reemergence. When something appeared that could steal away the hearts of His people, He knew that unless it was completely eradicated, it would simply come back stronger than ever—it would reemerge with formidable strength in their lives.

This is simply a principle of life experience. We've all seen this acted out many times.

You've finally lost weight, then you stop watching what you eat, and *boom*! You gain back more than you lost. After living sober for years, you take a few "casual" drinks, and the desire comes roaring back in, worse than before. You haven't had a cigarette in months, but after a weekend of thinking you can handle it, you find yourself dominated by the desire once again. You've finally built meaningful relationships, then things get busy and you stop going to small group and find yourself more isolated than ever.

Partial obedience sets the stage for reemergence every time.

Repeatedly, God told His people that if they didn't destroy everything as He instructed them, not only would they experience the fallout in their lives, but they would also watch the sins of the fathers be visited down to the third and fourth generations. Despite how it may sound to our twenty-first century ears, He spoke it less as a punishment and more as a reality of expected consequences. Partial obedience yields halfhearted followers. The generations to follow would end up worshipping the idols of the very enemies they had conquered. The God who loved them warned them, "A divided life will not only be *your* ruin, but also the heartache of those who follow after you." As a pastor, I have a special window into the lives of many, and I've seen this principle realized more times than I care to recall. I've seen it played out in the pain of divorce, addiction, materialism, pride,

> Partial obedience yields halfhearted followers.

entitlement, skepticism, lust, and insecurity . . . and that's just the beginning. When we don't deal with the divides in our hearts, we hand down destruction to our families. And the results are heartbreaking.

JOHN: A NEW INHERITANCE

A renowned judge in our city, John, came through the door of Quest as a "respected, upstanding, Christian family man." But underneath it all, John had a secret. Spiritual pride was keeping him from truly humbling himself before God. As a hypocrite, his example led his family to play the part, attend church, do devotions—all the while camouflaging an empty, lifeless existence in the grip of pride.

> *I thought I was a Christian my whole adult life, but I was bothered by the lack of evidence of Christ in my life. I had a huge ego, and comparison, performance, and pride were everyday companions. Everything in my life was centered around me.*
>
> *Running for office, I sized people up based on how they could help me—if they would put a sign in their yards, or put a bumper sticker on their cars, or donate money to my campaign. It was all about me and what they could do to help me. I felt like I was doing it for a noble purpose, I really did, but I realized over time that I was just trying to make people recognize me and respect me.*

As I compared myself to everyone, I came to realize that it was just a sham. If nothing else, I would claim to be more spiritual or more humble than the other person. And it was just ridiculous. That's what it came down to, and it was made worse because I was a judge. Everybody stands up when you come into the courtroom and they all laugh at your jokes, but it only made it more obvious to me that something was missing.

The problem is, the pride didn't stop there. Sin never does. It found its way into the lives of the people John loved the most—including his daughter Mary Alice. After years of trying, she found herself stuck in the same place, unable to make ground in her journey toward God.

Several years ago, all of that changed at an outdoor baptism. After hearing dozens of people share the incredible stories of Jesus' rescue in their lives, I gave the crowd the chance to respond and give their lives to Christ. Out of nowhere, I remember seeing the unthinkable—John was standing, humbling himself, ready to surrender his life to Christ.

Sensing the gravity of this moment—the public fall of pride—I interrupted the entire event to address John: "Tell me what you're doing, John."

"I'm tired of playing the part—I've got to give my life to Christ!" he called out, tears streaming down his face.

John was never the same after that night.

No one who truly encounters Christ ever is.

He's no longer marked by trying and performing and

striving. He rests in a relationship with the God who made him to love Him. And the good news doesn't end there. It took a few years, but after many prayers, a frank talk with her dad—who asked for forgiveness for his spiritual pride—and lots of caring and investing, Mary Alice finally humbled *herself* at the foot of the cross and gave *her* life to Christ.

Our idolatry passes destruction on to our children and their children, but God's grace is so far-reaching that our humility opens the door not only to *our* restoration, but to our children's as well.

GETTING TRACTION: HOW TO OVERTHROW AN IDOL

Almost no one sets out to live a double-minded life and intentionally wreck the lives of their children and their children's children. Instead, I think most of the time we have an encounter with God and we make our declarations to Him with sincerity, but we simply don't do the *necessary work* to overthrow our idols. Instead of destroying them, we merely wound them, exposing ourselves to the principle of reemergence.

So how can we actually destroy them? If you're ready to push play and take action, here are four clear steps to a full-force rebellion against the power of idols in your life:

1. Do the honest work of identifying your idols.

Name them. If you can't name your idols, you can't kill them or even effectively pray against them. If your willingness to make war is essentially just a vague sense of dissatisfaction with your spiritual life, it won't get you anywhere. Where is the Tiger Principle at work in your life? In other words, identify what you think you need to make you happy. What is your "Jesus *and . . .*"?

> Is there a dream, a wish, a need that has an inordinate pull on your life, that has the password to your soul?

Is there a dream, a wish, a need that has an inordinate pull on your life, that has the password to your soul? Or think of it like this: what phone call, text, or invitation could come and have the power to shake you to your core and tempt you to abandon your trust and reliance on God? If you can identify it, there may be an idol lurking there. But the good news is this: you are one step closer to overthrowing it.

2. Do the humbling work of grieving your unfaithfulness.

Sounds like fun, right? Don't mistake this for beating yourself up. There's a crucial step here.

When you gave your heart to Christ, you essentially said, "You're the One for me." But when you took on other "lovers" and began to worship them (by giving them power or depending on them), you traded "Jesus alone" for "Jesus *and . . .*" That exchange became a moment of relational infidelity to the One who loves you; the One who's never had a wandering eye or had a second thought about you. It's not about guilt—it's about relational reality. When we worship idols, we break the heart of God, because His love is perfect and His desire is for us to be fully and faithfully His. If we skip the work of grieving, we skip the reality that our actions matter to His heart. And sometimes, in our bid for "happiness," we break the heart of the Person who loves us most.

Here's an important distinction: true grieving isn't just being sad about being caught. A good friend of mine recently discovered that her father had been engaged in an affair for over a year. It is important to note that he didn't fess up—he got caught. In the following days, it became clear that he was really sad he got caught. He's sad that he's caused pain, drama, and tension in the family. He tells his wife, "I love you. This doesn't have to be a big deal. Let's just go back to the way it was, and everything will be good again." His words betray him: he has no real understanding as to what he's done. He hasn't scratched the surface of the relational destruction he has caused.

> Idolatry is indicative of an ongoing affair that has hurt the heart of the One who is devoted to you.

When someone expresses true sorrow— real repentance—it's undeniable. Whether through tears, words, or actions, it is obvious that they've begun to understand the depth of what they've done to hurt those around them.

Idolatry isn't just one sin among many. It's indicative of an ongoing affair that has hurt the heart of the One who is devoted to you. Do the work of grieving your unfaithfulness to God, who has never been unfaithful to you.

3. Do the violent work of destroying your idols.

This is a crucial action step. Without this step, the other steps are just talk. It leaves you impotent and unable to get any lasting traction with the first commandment.

We don't have many great pictures of idol destruction in the modern era. But you can get a glimpse if you know where to look. I suggest you search for the video of a now-famous moment: the destruction of a statue of Saddam Hussein by the Iraqi people. After years under his oppressive regime, the people of Iraq were finished with Hussein. But it wasn't enough to just overthrow his government, his rule, and his way of life;

> Some of you are in a full-blown affair with the "Jesus and . . ." in your life.

they took it a step further. In an unforgettable picture of liberty, they toppled the large statue of the evil dictator in the public square, announcing to the world, "The era of Saddam Hussein is done. He is overthrown and his influence destroyed."

This is exactly what we must do.

What will a forceful removal of this idol look like in your life?

It comes down to practical steps. What's your battle plan; what's the war you're ready to make? Some of you are in a full-blown affair with the "Jesus *and* . . ." in your life. End the relationship today. Throw something in the fire that needs to be destroyed. Quit the job that has stolen your heart and is stealing you from your family. Move from the neighborhood that only drags you into sin. Change your phone number, block some callers, filter some websites, or exchange your smartphone for a dumb one. I encourage you to do whatever it takes and refuse to keep this private; talk with someone close to you about how to take radical measures. Go on record, out loud with people who will call you on it.

Need more convincing? Take the word of a few of my friends:

John, who overthrew the idol of spiritual pride.
Lorrie, who defeated the idol of materialism.
Brian, who destroyed the idol of adultery.
Rachel, who obliterated the idol of approval.
Craig, who conquered the idol of self-protection.
Kay, who stopped idolizing her family.
Johannes, who defeated the idol of control.

Make your war plan. It's time for an active overthrow! What do you need to do to topple the idols in your life? Find a way to do it, announcing to the world, "Today, I make war. The era of this idol is over!"

> Make your war plan. It's time for an active overthrow!

4. Do the wise work of fortifying against your idols.

It's time to do whatever it takes to prevent the principle of reemergence. Enact what you learned in "Tipping Point"; this is where you employ PAR:

Position yourself well
Advance decision-making
Resolve to live a self-examined life

Warning: these idols won't go quietly; they'll fight to come back and return with far more force. So release the Romans 8:11 reality that Jesus died in order to pour supernatural strength into your life. The same Spirit that brought Jesus back to life lives inside you. If death didn't stand a chance against Him, do you think pornography does? Do you think alcohol, insecurity, eating disorders, greed, or pride stands a real chance of victory? The Spirit of God can decisively put the idol to death, but it's up to us to fortify against that idol's resuscitation in our life.

Fortification looks different in different situations.

In some cases, it means that you take a different route home from work because you can't drive past that club. You set up a plan: when you leave work, you call a trustworthy friend and talk from the minute you leave to the second you get home. Sound overdone? A little dramatic? Not if it overthrows the insidious work of idolatry in your life and the lives of your children. You're fortifying.

Some of you need to walk up to your boss and say, "I have a problem. You treat me really well, but gaining your approval has begun to mean too much. I'm going to be making some shifts in the way I work. I'm going to aim for excellence rather than approval."

Others of you may realize that the pursuit of money and possessions has gained a stranglehold on your mind and heart. In order to fortify and make God first in your finances, you may need to begin using auto-withdrawal for your tithe to your local church, to ensure that you're giving

God the first and the best of what He provides for you. You may need to sign up for a financial retraining course or get Christian financial counseling.

Some of you go to great churches and hear terrific Bible teaching, but weekly sermons aren't meant to be your only sustenance. In order to fortify your life with the Word of God, you need to begin to read His Word on your own, even five minutes a day. You may want to find a Bible study or a small group where you can continually explore and digest His Word.

Some of you have become so mired in a general sense of self-focus that you need to seek out opportunities to go and serve those in difficult situations. Whether it's a disaster relief trip, serving at a soup kitchen, or simply mowing a neighbor's lawn, do whatever will fortify your fidelity to God and your dependence on Him and undermine the power of the deceased idols in your life.

No matter how hard the idols fall, if you don't fortify, you'll be threatened again, maybe in months, maybe in years—perhaps when you least expect it. Fortify. It's a lynchpin in overthrowing your idols.

THE FINAL FRAME

Do you know that movies are often made completely out of sequence?

Commonly, the director will choose to film the last scene first. Why? To be sure they start with the end target in mind.

Do you want a spoiler of the final frame of our story? The book of Revelation describes a reality where Jesus is at the center of everything. There's no mention of houses, cars, designer clothes, romance, or anything else that tempts us with "Jesus *and* . . ." The final moments of the Bible are filled with overwhelming worship of the One who bears the marks of nails in His hands and feet, the scar of a spear in His side, and the wounds left by a crown of thorns.

In that last scene it seems unmistakably clear to each person: *He loves me! He's always been faithful and true, even when I haven't been. He volunteered His life to be in an exclusive relationship with me!*

> Overthrow the idols and exclusively worship the One who will always love you.

So begin with that end in mind. A faithful, exclusive, enduring "for-better-or-worse" relationship with Jesus!

Some of us have never known a full revelation of God because we've never had an idol-free season with Him. It's always been "Jesus *and* . . ."

You were made for more. And in your most honest reflections, it's becoming clear to you that while you may know a great deal about Jesus, maybe even believed the best about Him, you've yet to give Him your life—exclusively. You haven't opened the door; He hasn't made His home in your heart. You're close! In the next chapter, I pray you will give yourself wholeheartedly to Him.

"Choose this day whom you will serve."

Overthrow the idols and exclusively worship the One who will always love you.

It's time for action; it's time for a coup; it's time for freedom.

GETTING TRACTION

⏪ REWIND

What will ultimately reside at the center of my life, defining my sense of satisfaction and meaning? Can I be satisfied with Jesus alone?

⬇ DOWNLOAD

Choose for yourselves this day whom you will serve. . . . As for me and my household, we will serve the LORD. JOSHUA 24:15, NIV

▶ PUSH PLAY

Analyze and determine the idols in your life, take hold of God's power and reject them, and then fortify against them.

Chapter 10

RUN TO HIM

I LOVE BEING with my boys. They make everything better, every hang time an adventure, and every day more filled with gratitude. Needless to say, when I have to be away from them on business, I always count down the minutes until I'm back with them again.

I remember one time in particular after a lengthy business trip when I just couldn't wait to get home. Corey, my oldest son, was four at the time, bursting with "off-the-charts" energy levels and scarcely "on-the-charts" obedience levels (must have gotten it from his mother). As a result, he and I had made an "arrangement" before I left: he would obey his mom quickly, go to bed without a fight, and not tackle any of his friends when they weren't looking. In short, Corey was going to be *good* while I was gone. But by the time I returned from my trip, our "arrangement" was honestly the last thing on my mind; I was just looking forward to seeing my son. When I breezed through the front door, tossing suitcase and car keys aside, I was eager to see him—to hug and hold him and tell him how much I loved and missed him.

Immediately, I heard him yelling from his seat at the kitchen table. "Daaaddy!" followed by the sound of four-year-old feet hitting the hardwood floor. As he made the sharp right turn into the hallway, the socks he was wearing started to work against his speed. He careened through doorways and slid into every available surface. I watched him zoom into sight, exuberantly sliding into and then bouncing off of the nearest wall. In true Instagram fashion, I knelt on one knee and flung my arms wide open to receive the embrace of my firstborn.

But instead of that timeless moment, I watched Corey's countenance suddenly change as he made eye contact with me. Rather than joyful eyes and a smiling face, his brow furrowed and his face fell. He hit the brakes and came to a screeching stop, halting about two steps from me. Before I could figure out his strange welcome or utter a word, Corey was sharing his heart in a single sentence, as only a four-year-old can:

"Daddy . . . I was *not* good."

It didn't matter that I was dying to see him, that I loved him far beyond whatever had happened at home, or that right now, I just wanted to be with my son. In Corey's mind, being "not good" superseded our relationship. His "not goodness" was all he could see, and he assumed it was all I saw too.

WHAT GOD KNOWS

Do you realize that God knows everything about you? He knows what you did and said last night. He knows that secret you have been keeping for years. He knows the dreams and half-baked ideas that have skated through your mind when you were barely even paying attention. He knows every choice you have made (see Hebrews 4:13).

Just to go ahead and make it worse: God knows the evil you will do in the future. The people you'll use and hurt, the lies you'll tell, the promises you'll break—even to Him. God is never away on a trip; He knows it all right now. He knows when we've been "not good." The craziest part? He's known it *forever*!

But God is more than a glorified Santa Claus who "knows if we've been bad or good." He *knows* you completely, and in the midst of all that, He's absolutely nuts about you! He really does love you with all your junk. No matter how bad it gets. No matter what you said, what you smoked, how much you drank, or what you watched.

He loves you. Know why? Because He made you! You are no accident to Him—you were carefully planned for. God crafted you with His own hands. In fact, Psalm 139:13 tells us that He was there with you in the womb. He looked into your eyes before your mom or dad ever could, and He adored you there. This psalm goes on to say that He made you carefully and tenderly—you are His masterpiece.

True, others might look at you and not see all that God sees. Their assessment may fall far short of His, but that's simply their opinion. God designed you for greatness. And no matter what brokenness may be unearthed in your

> **God made you carefully and tenderly— you are His masterpiece.**

Transformation Adventure, God has never lost sight of His original design for you. He made you special . . . one of a kind to make a one-of-a-kind difference with your life *now*; to trust Him and step out, not waiting for "someday" to exercise your God-given gifts and qualities.

However, we often look in the mirror and see only the brokenness. We focus on our mistakes, regrets, failures. And when that's our perspective, we hide, protect, run, and cover up the truth. We assume that the last thing He would want is for us to run into His arms.

Sound familiar?

From an early age, it gets into our heads that since God is so good, we'll never measure up. No matter how hard we try, much of the time we are simply "*not* good." So, like Corey, we skid to a stop before we get too close to Him, thinking "I'd better not go near Him until I get my act together."

That's certainly what I thought growing up. My mom went to church, and occasionally I would go with her. When I did, I would smile and try to put on a convincing performance, but I was waiting for lightning to strike or for the cross to fall off the building and hit me in the head. I even feared that the pastor would come after me with a Super Soaker full of holy water if the truth about me got out.

I was not a good kid.

I started young. Once for "show and tell," I wanted to liven things up a bit, so I got creative. In my humble opinion, I thought we needed more excitement in the classroom. Acting in that spirit—wanting to serve my fellow classmates and, of course, my teacher—I brought a bucket of live garter snakes to class and threw them into the room.

The other students loved it.

My teacher didn't.

The principal *really* didn't.

My bad behavior only escalated from there. I didn't obey my folks very well; I was constantly in trouble with everybody—parents, school personnel, police. I was an equal opportunity disrupter. I spent most of my sixth-grade year sitting at my desk in the closet—the only place Mr. Dole could put me where I wouldn't disrupt the class.

The desire for nonstop fun led me deep into brokenness very early in life. I saw things I never should have seen and did things I could never undo. Worst of all, I became a user. A user of people, of friends, of women—a user of anything that made me feel good. I did just about anything I could in the name of my own personal happiness. I didn't go out of my way to hurt people, but if it happened . . . that's the way it went. I did whatever made me feel good, and I did it on my own terms. This led me to dark and destructive places, interrupted by the occasional church trip with mom, where I smiled and played the part.

In one respect, it looked like I had it all—I had friends continually around me, I played football, and I enjoyed the perks of high school fun without much of a conscience. At the same time, I was going bankrupt internally—with no purpose and increasing emptiness, becoming more and more of a slave as I tried to fill the relentless hole in my heart. I was living out the story of the Prodigal Son.

FAR FROM HOME

A boy decides to leave home in pursuit of his own happiness. Jesus tells the parable in Luke 15. In just a few paragraphs, this story paints an incredible picture of the heart of God.

One of the reasons I love this story is what prompted Jesus to tell it in the first place. A bunch of religious people are giving Jesus a hard time, complaining and criticizing His methods. Jesus doesn't just "turn the other cheek" or let it go. He comes back with a tone that must have caught them off guard. It is as if He is saying, "So you really wanna understand God? You really wanna know His heart? Then let Me make it unmistakably clear to you."

The story in Luke 15 begins with a shocking pronouncement. The younger son of a father demands his inheritance on the spot. Those listening to Jesus knew how inheritances worked in their culture. A father would hold on to all the land, cattle, riches, and belongings he had earned over a lifetime and on his deathbed ceremoniously pass the bulk of it over to his oldest son, with smaller portions divided among his younger sons. That's the way it had always been done.

The younger son didn't care how it had always been done. "Hey, Dad, I know you've broken your back your whole life to build up this property and these possessions, but I'm entitled to them. Who cares about tradition? Sure, it will cause you deep embarrassment in the community when I start selling off the family land and livestock so that I can raise some cash. I know it will look like I just couldn't wait for you to die so that I could get my hands on your stuff. You and I both know I'm gonna blow your money on the trip I'm planning, but I really want it now!"

I don't know about your dad, but I can tell you that a first-century Middle Eastern dad would never stand for this kind of insolence. That kid is going to get it, and everyone listening knows it. In their culture, the father would be well within his rights to severely punish this disrespectful young son, and no one would have blamed him or even batted an eye. Jesus' audience couldn't wait for Him to get to that part of the story.

Instead, Jesus blows them away with the father's response: "Okay, Son, I can't stop you. I can't force you to stay. I'll divide up my property and give you your share early." Then presumably the father just stands back and watches this kid sell their family's prized possessions so he can raise cash, fill his pockets full, and then head out for the big city.

It's funny the things we do when we think we can get away with them. Can you think of something you've done that you feel guilty about? A lie you told, the time you used someone for your own gain, the decision you made to cheat, or the lust you indulged in? It's crazy how clearly you can feel the way your sinful choices separate you from God and others.

Well, this kid feels separated all right. He's got a pocket full of cash, and he starts partying like he's in Vegas. To translate "wild living" to twenty-first-century America, this kid takes his dad's life savings to MTV's *Spring Break* and goes crazy! It's like the first ever episode of *Jewish Boys Gone Wild*!

But the bright lights and big-city thrills don't last forever, and when his pockets are empty, life hits this kid hard in the face. His full-tilt days of wild living come to an abrupt end—in a pigpen. He is barely surviving in a job feeding pigs. It is the last place in the world he ever dreamed he'd end up, and it brings him to the end of his rope. Covered in mud and slop, he finds himself thinking, *How did I end up here . . . so alone in such a dark place?*

STUCK

No one ever intends to go so far off track. It is never the plan. No one has one drink and intends to become an alcoholic. No one cheats on a quiz and intends to become a lifelong fraud. No one tells a little white lie expecting to lie his or her way through life. No one flirts with someone he isn't married to intending to destroy the lives of the people he loves most. But it often happens this way, following the same principle: every great fall is preceded by a series of small missteps. This young Jewish boy was buried in the wreckage of his great fall.

So what do you do when you've gone so far, pretended so long, feel so bad and so unworthy? What do you do when you've distanced yourself from family, friends, and God by big mistakes that are gnawing at you?

Some of you are stuck just like the prodigal; you are eager to advance on your Transformation Adventure, but you're stuck in a distant place and you're in danger of slipping farther away. Some of you are stuck in drugs or pornography, and you can't stop using or stop acting on your fantasies. Some of you are stuck because you've cheated on your spouse, and now your marriage, your family, and your heart are a wreck.

> Every great fall is preceded by a series of small missteps.

But some of you are keeping a different kind of secret just beneath the surface. You're stuck in the church scene, trying to be good enough for God or someone else; stuck pretending that you're a follower of Jesus, but you know you are faking it. Things look good on the outside, but honestly things on the inside just aren't adding up. And every attempt to "do it right" leaves you tired and empty, feeling as far away from God as you could be.

What if, like the Prodigal Son, Jesus knows right where you are and intends to meet you at this crossroads in your life? Suppose that here in this stuck place, the One who died on the cross is offering you His love and forgiveness. The One who made you to love you wants to give you His grace, adopt you, and make you His own. God isn't angry with you like you may have expected. It's as if you are in a distant land like the Prodigal Son, yet, unbeknownst to you, God is actually fighting to get you home to Himself.

THE FATHER WHO RUNS

When I think of the fight God puts up for us, His wayward kids, I can't help but retell a story I heard from a missionary in Africa that illustrates the relentless heart of God as He pursues us:

> God isn't angry with you like you may have expected. He is actually fighting to get you home to Himself.

> *Several years ago my family and I were traveling from the Ivory Coast to Mali. Along the way we decided to stop beside the road and buy some fruit for our missionary friends. As I pulled in, I said to my wife, "Why don't you buy what you want, and I'll sit here in the car with the kids?"*
>
> *While she shopped, I kept the car and the air conditioner running full blast, trying to keep up with the hot African sun. About that time a vehicle pulled in behind us, and three armed men jumped out. The door on my side was ripped open, and a handgun was shoved against the side of my head.*

I remember looking in his eyes as the man said to me, "Do you want to die?"

All I could think about in that moment was how to save my family. So I grabbed my nearest daughter and literally threw her from the vehicle. As I began to yell at the top of my lungs for help, one of the men grabbed my arm and yanked me out. Then all three men jumped in my car, with my oldest son and my youngest daughter still inside.

As they slammed the doors and squealed away, I stumbled to my feet. The despair and helplessness I felt as I watched the car containing my two children race away cannot be put into words. I cried out to God from the depths of my heart, "Lord, how am I ever going to get them back?"

Then it happened. I looked down the road, and one hundred yards ahead was a police post. After initially driving toward it, the car made a sudden U-turn and actually started driving back in my direction. And in that instant, I saw that all hope wasn't lost. I had a brief moment to make a difference in the lives of my children. So with everything I had, I sprinted across the median to the other side of the road. I dove, just missing the car, but somehow managed to grab onto the spare tire strapped to the back of it.

As they sped along, I pulled myself up. I could see my son through the rear window—weeping, screaming, and trying to do anything to get out. I remember the thought going through my mind, "Lord, today is a good day to die, and this is a good purpose to die for. I will give myself for my children."

Friend, this is God's heart for you—no matter who you are or what you have done. That is the kind of relentless love that is in hot pursuit of all of us. It's the story of the Cross—the Father doing all He can to get His kids back from distant places. God is willing to pursue you through your pride, insecurity, and pretending. He'll do anything to prove His love to you if you'll let your defenses down and surrender to His outstretched, nail-pierced hands. He is chasing after you in the midst of every circumstance you face.

Wonder what happened to the missionary and his family? By the grace of God, he hung on and refused to be shaken loose from the car. The men realized that this wasn't going to be as easy as they'd planned. They slammed on the brakes, and all three men jumped out and abandoned the vehicle (perhaps in fear of the approaching police). Both children were recovered safe and unharmed.

The missionary was ready to give up his life to save his kids. But in the last possible second, his life was spared. The Bible tells a different story about our own rescue. There was no intervention, no last-minute escape for God's only Son. The One who went running for us died to set us free. The apostle Paul explains it well: "God declared an end to sin's control over us by giving his Son as a sacrifice for our sins" (Romans 8:3).

THE OFFER OF A LIFETIME

Do you know what happened to the Prodigal Son? Luke 15:17 records six of the most incredibly freeing words ever written: "He finally came to his senses." Those six words changed everything. In that gracious moment of clarity, he stood up and ran to his father. And do you know the craziest part? It says that the father was watching for him—not to scold, but to forgive, embrace, and welcome his long-lost boy home.

When I was fifteen and far from God, I experienced my own "six-word moment" when a man told me that Jesus would forgive me. Despite the broken, sinful places I had come from, he said that Jesus would come into my heart if I would just open the door. I came to my senses enough to recognize the incredible offer being extended to me. I didn't weigh it out or second-guess it—I simply ran to Him!

Like me, countless men and women I know—sons and daughters in faraway places—have followed the example of the prodigal, finally realizing in a blast of clarity exactly what they needed to do. Doctors and drug dealers, churchgoers and adulterers, stay-at-home moms and gang members. The offer of God's grace is available to literally *everyone*. Maybe my friend Sandra's story will help you marvel even more at the heart of a lovesick Father.

Sandra found herself trapped in a prison of self-gratification and addiction. After years of alcoholism, drug use, two abortions, two failed marriages, and a career in the adult entertainment industry, Sandra was bankrupt—emotionally, financially, relationally, and most painfully of all, spiritually. She had experienced rejection in her church and therefore had assumed that God had rejected her too. In light of the life she had lived, it didn't seem like a stretch to believe that.

But in an unexpected moment of clarity, Sandra came to her senses. She decided to give church one more try, and instead of being judged, she found a place where she was welcomed and valued—and where the truth of God's love and grace finally became clear. She understood the Father's heart for her for the first time, and in her own "six-word moment," she ran to Him. He received her with open arms. Sandra found the grace, freedom, and forgiveness that Jesus was offering her. These days His love literally spills out of her in worship, in the way she serves, and in the ways she helps other prodigals come home. She can't stop telling people about the Father who pursued her with His love. Sandra spends the best hours of her days as a rescuer. She helps women who are stuck in the sex trade industry like she used to be. Her life is a beacon of hope to everyone who, like the Prodigal, finds themselves in a distant land.

> Everyone who runs to God makes it every single time.

Do you know what Psalm 18:30 says? "Everyone who runs toward him makes it" (*The Message*). Everyone who runs to God makes it every single time. He's never rejected anyone—ever. Just ask my son, Carson, who on September 6, 2009, heard the words, "You're never too young and you're never too old to give your life to Christ" and decided to do just that. So can you. The Father is scanning the horizon right now—searching, watching, and praying to see you. He wants to welcome you, forgive you, and adopt you as His own.

You were designed to make a difference, to change the world. But before God makes a difference *through* you, He wants to make a difference *in* you. Let Him change you by filling you with His Spirit, giving you power like you've never known. With His power loosed within, you'll discover the strength to forgive, to trust, and to risk.

There is no need to remain in distant places any longer, my friend. He made you to love you. Isn't it time to get brutally honest and admit that you need Him? Isn't it time to head home?

Why would you wait any longer? You can simply run to Him.

From your loneliness . . . *run to Him.*
From your fear . . . *run to Him.*
From your doubt . . . *run to Him.*
From your lust . . . *run to Him.*
From your guilt . . . *run to Him.*
From your anger . . . *run to Him.*
From your unforgiveness . . . *run to Him.*
From your regret . . . *run to Him.*
From your insecurity . . . *run to Him.*
From your pride . . . *run to Him.*

What life are you waiting for? As the eyes of God search and the angels of heaven cheer you on . . . run to Him! I'll guide you with a simple prayer like millions and millions across history have prayed to God as they have invited Him to make His home in their hearts. If you're ready to run to Him, say these words:

Father, thank You for loving me.

Thank You for not giving up on me, but pursuing me in distant places.

I want to come home today. I want to give You my whole heart, once and for all.

I believe that Jesus died on the cross in my place.

Please forgive my sins. I am truly sorry for the ways I've ignored You and gone my own way.

I accept the gift of Your forgiveness and grace.

Jesus, I invite You to come into my heart. I give You my life.

Today, I am running into Your arms.

I receive You as my Savior and the Leader of my life.

Fill me with Your Holy Spirit and help me follow You forever.

I am Yours from this day forward.

I pray this prayer from the bottom of my heart.

In Jesus' name, Amen.

Congratulations! You've made the best and most important single decision of your entire life and eternity. You have accepted the deal of a lifetime. John 1:12 says, "But to all who believed him and accepted him, he gave the right to become children of God."

Now rest in your decision and His promise of forgiveness and love. You belong to God now! Be yourself as a freshly redeemed, dearly loved child of the Most High God. Let Him lead you down your Grace Path. You are in for quite a Transformation Adventure, my friend. Remember, the same Spirit who raised Jesus from the dead is now alive and activated in you. Cooperate. Trust Him. He has you, and you have Him.

Buckle up as the life you were made for has just begun! Welcome home.

GETTING TRACTION

⏪ REWIND

God's not angry with you. He's never lost sight of His original design for you. You are His masterpiece.

⬇ DOWNLOAD

Everyone who runs toward him makes it.
PSALM 18:30, *THE MESSAGE*

▶ PUSH PLAY

Admit where you are far from God and run to Him.

Chapter 11

PUSH PLAY NOW

LAST SUMMER the Quest worship team was on a retreat at a beautiful Tennessee lake. During a break, a few members of the team found something potentially fun: a homemade rope swing, dangling from a tree branch over the water. One by one, the team members summoned their courage, swung out, and felt the adrenaline rush of a twenty-foot drop into the water. The rest of us who hadn't been there had to listen to their stories, which quickly morphed from the creaky rope swing into a fifty-foot Special Forces drop into piranha-infested water.

My family and I, along with some close friends, went to the lake later in the summer. While we were cruising along in a pontoon boat, I spotted the rope swing. It hung from a towering old tree. The rope was frayed, and it had a crude, homemade handle. No wonder the lake leapers had exaggerated their reports. Justin, who had survived the earlier antics, looked at the lake and was wary about repeating his performance. Yes, it was the same rope swing, but it wasn't the same lake. The water had receded at least five feet, increasing the free-fall time considerably but shortening the distance to the bottom of the lake. Still it was irresistible.

"How about it? Is anyone in?" I asked enthusiastically.

Silence.

And then, with all the chutzpah an eight-year-old can muster, Carson spoke up.

"*I'll* do it!"

The gauntlet was thrown down, and some accepted the challenge. But the journey wasn't for the faint of heart.

Leaving the boat behind and swimming to the hill, the would-be rope swingers had to walk on sharp rocks covering the shore, contend with swarming bees and biting horseflies, and then make the steep climb up eroding cliffs (with wet bare feet). Once there, the task was clear: grab the handle, try not to throw up, and then—hanging on for dear life—run forward, only letting go when the swing reached its maximum arc.

Gravity did the rest.

The adults went first, showing the kids how to swing and release over the water. One by one, the older kids started following, each working up the courage to make the plunge. Seasoned rope-swinger Justin stood on the shore, yelling to each kid, "Let go!" when they reached the perfect trajectory.

Eventually it was Carson's turn. He wanted to do it, but it

was daunting even for an adult, much less the youngest of the group by far. Everyone was shouting encouragement his way.

Gathering his nerve, Carson gripped the handle and began to run forward, and then he started to let go—before even leaving the ground! Justin grabbed him before he toppled over the cliff onto the rocks below. I'm not sure who was more rattled—Carson or Justin.

Another round of coaching began. "Carson, you can't let go until you're told to," Justin counseled him, "but when you're told, you have to! If you don't hang on until I say 'Let go!' then I can't be held responsible for what happens!" (Translated: "I will not be responsible for letting my pastor's son die on the rocks.") While I appreciated the sentiment, I decided to speak up.

"Carsi, you can do this, buddy! I totally believe in you. You've got this. But you must let go exactly when you're supposed to, right? And hey, Carsi—if you don't want to do this, you know you don't have to, okay? We all love you and believe in you, big-time. Your call—I'm with you all the way!"

I watched his little hands tighten their grip on the handle.

"I'm going to go for it, Dad!"

For all the waiting, warnings, and coaching, it came down to this. It was Carson's moment.

Like a pro, he sprinted forward, pulled his legs up, and soared out over the water. Justin shouted, "Let go!" and he did! He was a fifty-pound human cannonball, hitting the water in perfect form. He came up grinning and laughing, pumping his right fist in the air, shouting, "That was *awesome*!" Cheers erupted from across the lake.

It's a moment Carson will never forget, because he's the one who chose to go for it. He alone could step into what would prove to be one of the most exhilarating rides of his short lifetime, or make a choice that would leave him wishing and waiting for someday. After giving him a big hug, I said, "What finally gave you the courage to take the leap?"

> You will *never* be here again. You can never recover this moment. You will either seize it or waste it.

"I had to, Dad. What if I'm never here again?"

Well put. What if *you* are never here again? Clarification: you will *never* be here again. You can never recover this moment. Each day, each season, each year comes to us only once. And when it's gone, it vanishes into the past.

You will either seize it or waste it; you'll make the most of it or watch it fade into the distance, wondering what might have been. I want to help those of you who are tired of watching and waiting, sick to death of living your lives on pause. I am praying with all my might that you will hear me yelling, "Let go!" and experience the thrill of soaring as you finally *push play now* on the life you were meant to live.

GETTING OUT OF THE BOAT

Things change when we jump. God's supernatural power works in conjunction with our willingness to let Him ignite our courage to step out. This is not only possible, but it finds precedent in some familiar places in the Gospels. Let's revisit an old friend and borrow some courage.

Have you ever wondered why Jesus picked the apostle Peter to be part of His inner circle? What was it about the fisherman from Capernaum that made him a candidate for such an influential role—preacher of the first sermon about Jesus, leader of the first church, the one to whom God gave "the keys of the Kingdom of Heaven" (Matthew 16:19)?

> He may not have always moved in the right direction, but Peter always moved.

Jesus' recruiting criteria is never laid out in Scripture, so here are my two cents: I think He loved that Peter always initiated action. He may not have always moved in the right direction, but Peter always moved. He wasn't simply a dreamer who talked a lot and did little. He was someone who pursued the heart of God with an "act first, think later" mentality. Throughout the Gospels, you see Peter constantly in motion—"Let me go first. . . . I have an answer. . . . Take me with You. . . . I'm in." Essentially Peter's heart boiled down to this: "I may not be all that qualified, but I'm ready." I think part of the reason you and I know Peter's name today is because he initiated audacious action. Let's learn from a world-class example of this: Peter's legendary stroll on the Sea of Galilee recorded in Matthew 14.

Meanwhile, the disciples were in trouble far away from land, for a strong wind had risen, and they were fighting heavy waves. About three o'clock in the morning Jesus came toward them, walking on the water. When the disciples saw him walking on the water, they were terrified. In their fear, they cried out, "It's a ghost!"

But Jesus spoke to them at once. "Don't be afraid," he said. "Take courage. I am here!"

Then Peter called to him, "Lord, if it's really you, tell me to come to you, walking on the water."

"Yes, come," Jesus said.

So Peter went over the side of the boat and walked on the water toward Jesus.

MATTHEW 14:24–29

This is classic Peter. We can imagine the other disciples in the boat yelling at him to stop, and perhaps his younger brother, Andrew, grabbing his robe to deter him. I bet as one foot went over the edge of the boat and onto the raging water, Peter wondered, *How in the world did I get myself into this? What was I thinking, "Tell me to come to You"?* But he didn't stop and turn back.

JUST SAY THE WORD

When it comes to risk-taking, I've known many people who overthink to the point of doing nothing. They consider the risk so thoroughly that at the end of the day they are standing in the very same spot where they started. This isn't a big deal when it concerns your landscaping or a new hobby. But when the plans of God are at stake, there is a very real price to pay for inactivity. Are you an overthinker or a person who takes action? With Peter, it's a forgone conclusion what he will do.

What happened in this brief interaction between Peter and Jesus is an invaluable lesson to those on the Transformation Adventure. Jesus does not force Peter out of the boat, nor will He force you. He will not make you put your faith into action. He won't do it; it's not His style. Jesus offers divine possibility and the freedom to pick. It was Peter's choice.

> When the plans of God are at stake, there is a very real price to pay for inactivity.

Don't overlook what's clearly in the text: Peter *asked* Jesus to call him onto the water. He wasn't the only disciple in the boat. Any one of the others could have made that daring request, but only Peter did.

"Lord, You call me and I'll come. Just say the word!"

"Come," Jesus replied.

Can you imagine, for a moment, Jesus' smile? Peter actually gets out of a perfectly good boat, planting his feet gingerly on water that suddenly feels like solid ground. His eyes are locked on Jesus.

What did Jesus' eyes look like in that moment? No one knows for sure, but I'm betting that they were shining— brimming over with sheer joy and excitement. *This hotheaded fisherman is actually bold enough and filled with enough faith to get out of that boat and trust Me!* Despite the rather famous sinking incident that followed, for a moment Jesus' eyes must have been sparkling.

The same is true of how He looks at you and me today. Every time someone gets out of the boat and risks courageous faith, Jesus' eyes brim with possibility. *All right! Another Peter. Someone with risky faith. That's what I'm talking about!* It's more than being willing. Like Peter, you must take the initiative and actually step out. Wishing and waiting never changes the world. Faith becomes genuine when it's put into action. It's those who exercise audacious faith that God uses to make an impact.

> Wishing and waiting never changes the world. Faith becomes genuine when it's put into action.

By His power, you can do this, but you will have to choose it. If you do, Jesus will meet you on the water. I promise you, there is something important that the Lord has planned for you this very day, and He wants you to be fearless in seizing that opportunity. You won't know in advance how it all plays out—Peter didn't. But you'll never know until you demonstrate the faith to start. And when you do, you will almost immediately begin to feel the exhilaration of having begun your adventure with the Savior.

HE'S NEVER DROPPED ANYONE

What does stepping over the side of the boat look like for you? It could mean you stop just talking about that vision God's planted into your heart and you take the first step to enact it. Perhaps it's time to forgive the people who wronged you so long ago and let them off the hook. Tomorrow you text someone and set up lunch to ask the hard question. By the end of the week you talk with your boss about working less so you can begin serving more. Take action now: get counseling, admit your issue, apologize to your spouse, confess your secret, write that check, reach out to your neighbor, become a follower of Christ.

Regardless of what your courageous step is, one thing is certain: you can trust the One who calls you. He has never dropped anyone—not one time. In Christ, you are a beloved child of the Most High God. You have been redeemed by the blood of Jesus. If the same Spirit that raised Him from the dead lives in you, don't you think He is able to sustain you in the deepest, most tumultuous water?

You may be thinking, *You don't know me or my situation, the circumstances and challenges I face.* But Jesus does, and He is calling you to Himself, out in faith territory. God is absolutely aware of your heart, relationships, fears, and issues. He knows you and your life even better than you do.

> What place of safety and security are you clinging to rather than stepping out with your eyes on Jesus?

What place of safety and security are you clinging to rather than stepping out with your eyes on Jesus? Can you identify the boat He's calling you to climb out of? Here's a clue: it's probably safe, comfortable, and familiar. In Matthew 14, the disciples' boat was their home away from home; but they were caught in a storm, and it was in trouble. It may have even been sinking, yet they wanted to stay in it. They were afraid for their lives, yet they didn't want to get out. With two choices before them—listen to the voice of fear and remain in a boat that might possibly sink, or exercise faith and step out onto the open water with Jesus (who *wasn't* sinking)—eleven of the twelve stuck with fear.

What's keeping you in your sinking boat today? What fear has hold of you? *What will my friends say if I step out? How will I manage my life and schedule? Will I still be able to pursue the plans I have for my future? What if I fail? Do I have what it takes to trust Him?*

Can you name the anxiety that has frozen faith out and anchored fear in? Once you've identified the enemy that stands between you and trusting Christ, whisper out loud the name above all names: *Jesus.* Ask for His help, ask for His strength, and then, with your eyes locked on His, move . . . step . . . go over the edge of the boat. That's where Jesus is! Friends, to expand upon Nelson Mandela's phrase that "Courage isn't the absence of fear," I say courage is taking action in the face of fear.

> Can you name the anxiety that has frozen faith out and anchored fear in?

Take a concrete action step away from the safe confines of your boat and move toward Him. Don't sit down at the table and negotiate with your fears. They only want to talk you into editing yourself out of the grand plans God has for your life. Become uncomfortable with your complacency. Stop being afraid of what will happen if you step out onto the water and start being bothered by what will never happen if you *don't*.

UNLIKELY HEROES

You can do this! I have seen the most unlikely people step out and accomplish incredible things for Christ.

My wife, Jacki, and I sat down at Buckhead restaurant with Dan and Laura. Over dinner I did my best to cast a compelling vision for giving our all to start a church radically committed to reaching and loving wayward sons and daughters. I wanted Dan and Laura to become pioneers with us in this far-reaching endeavor for Jesus. I could offer no promise of success. I gave them no guarantee that this would be easy on their young family of five, or even fruitful for that matter. Their response is permanently etched in my memory. Without hesitation, Dan looked me in the eye and said, "I'm way ahead of you. When do we start?" Fifteen years later they are still lead volunteers advancing the cause of Christ in the church they helped pioneer.

Anyerin and Jamie Lea refused to listen to fear as they waved good-bye to their family in Australia, boarded an airplane headed halfway around the world to America when they were expecting their first child—all because Jesus called them. God is using their lives, and Anyerin is leading thousands to the cross in worship each week.

My wife, Jacki, used to be scared to death of people who didn't know Christ. But when she stepped out of the boat, Jesus did spiritual surgery and broke her heart with love that transformed her into an irrepressible lover of those far from God.

Lindsey followed Jesus out into turbulent water and chose

to forgive the man who raped her, even praying that Jesus would lead him to her church so he might find forgiveness and hope for himself.

Connie lives outside of the boat, trading away her dream of doting solely on her children as a stay-at-home mom. She serves sacrificially as a high-capacity volunteer at Quest, which is hours from her home. She leads a team of researchers to help messages be the best they can be. She's impacting more lives than she previously could have imagined. Her example is transforming and growing her daughters as God is using their mom to change the world.

Ken and Jess Land quit their jobs, sold their belongings, and moved their family of five on simple faith that God had called them to Kentucky. Now, three years later, they are leading a thriving church in Frankfort.

And there's my dad, Phil—in my prayers for twenty-three years—a stubborn long shot who finally got out of his boat, pronouncing, "Okay, I'm ready." He humbled himself as he surrendered and responded to Jesus' invitation to follow Him into uncharted water!

I love these people and their stories. They've stepped out of fear and into the invitation to join Jesus out on the water. But something is missing: *your* story. Your name needs to be added to the list of those who pushed play and followed Jesus into His rich plans for their lives.

Down through the ages far more attention has been paid to the fact that Peter eventually sank in the waves, as opposed to focusing on the fact that he walked on water. I think we are missing a key point. Rather than give Matthew 14:22-33 the heading "Jesus Walks on Water," I suggest we rename it "Peter Walks on Water"! Yes, Peter could have walked with his eyes on Jesus and never sunk, but it was also Peter's small faith that empowered him to throw down the gauntlet before Jesus in the first place. His small faith then got him over the edge of the boat and propelled him to actually walk on water that historic day. I bet Peter *never* forgot that experience. In fact, I guarantee that it shaped his Transformation Adventure for the rest of his life.

> It's always better to be out on the water with Jesus than in the boat without Him.

I don't know what your next step is, but I can promise you this: it's always better to be out on the water with Jesus than in the boat without Him. As John Ortberg says, "If you want to walk on water, you've got to get out of the boat." You will never know the exhilaration of partnering with God to do the impossible until you lock eyes with Jesus and take action that formatively changes you from the inside out. It has the power to rewrite entire chapters along your Transformation Adventure.

IT'S NOT TOO LATE

I've been a pastor for more than twenty years, and I understand well some of the challenges to taking faith-filled action steps in the right direction. As a brand-new Christian back in 1982, I took the words of Ephesians 2:10 to heart, captured in the music of Christian artist Keith Green:

We are His workmanship, created for good works
in Christ.

He calls us to offer up ourselves a living sacrifice.

I recall talking to the Lord from the bottom of my heart,
saying, "That's exactly who I want to be and what I want to
do, Jesus. I want to be a living sacrifice who faithfully lives
out every single good work You have planned for me to do."

I'm still saying that to Jesus more than three decades
later—from the bottom of my heart. Only these days I'm
not sitting alone and praying while Keith Green blasts from
a Sanyo car stereo in my 1978 Ford Mustang II; I'm standing
in the vast company of countless other rescued people, joining my voice in worship to the One True God.

I've learned something very important about people
who've been rescued by Jesus and find their firm footing in
Him. At our best, we really want to live our lives to His glory,
fulfilling all the plans and dreams He has for us. We say it,
sing it, and write about it in journals, books, and blogs. But
in the end, if something doesn't click—if we don't *do* something about it—many of us become observers as the years
pass. We are more affected by the wind and the waves than
we are by God calling us out onto the water. We sit with the
eleven instead of stepping out with Peter.

You may recall the divine appointment I told you about
back in chapter 2. I regard that day sitting in Willow Creek
Community Church in 1997 as one of the most important
moments of my life. With God's help, I pushed play instantly

and stumbled onto my Grace Path, and He has been blowing my mind ever since.

Another person was sitting at Willow that day who played a significant role in my divine encounter. He was a total stranger to me. In fact, I still don't know his name. While hearing God call me out onto the water to begin a church, I remember looking over my shoulder and glancing behind me. Across the aisle a few rows back I saw a distinguished man in his late fifties or early sixties. He was dressed in a suit, holding a briefcase on his lap, and he was crying. Not bawling, but man-crying—red face, wide tear-filled eyes, and profound emotion.

While I watched him, he abruptly turned his face to me. I was caught. I felt bad about staring, but I couldn't turn away. Without exchanging a word, this man began to communicate with me. We must have stared at each other for twenty seconds, and in that time we had an entire conversation. He poured out his heart to me through his eyes: "Don't waste one word that you are hearing, Son. Don't blow it off. Don't think of all the reasons why it's too much, too difficult, or too risky. Listen to me: I missed my shot, I played it safe, I didn't go out onto the water, I stayed in the boat, and now it's too late. I said no and watched as others lived out the great plans God had for them. Don't follow in my footsteps. You don't want to live with this regret."

Friend, I want to say to you what I wished I could've said to him: *It's not too late.* If you're not dead, God's not done! You are here in the final pages of what has turned out to be a halftime speech—compelling, provoking, daring you by the power of the same Spirit that raised Jesus from the dead to be the person in Christ you have always wanted to be! Know what "halftime" means? It means that half the game still remains to be played. The time has come to push play on the life you've been waiting, yes longing, for! You are equipped to not only face the beast of wishing and waiting, of fear and insecurity, of anxiety and worry—but to slay him!

CARSON'S REVENGE

Last spring, my family and I received a great gift from my staff—free passes to Sea World! We were looking forward to revisiting some of our favorite attractions as well as scoping out some of the new ones. But for my youngest son, Carson, this trip to Sea World was a long-awaited showdown.

Why? For years, Carson has made war on height. He's had an ongoing battle with the "You Must Be This Tall To Ride" sign at the entrance to the thrill rides. For all our family's memory-making trips to theme parks, Carson hadn't enjoyed them as much as the rest of us had. Instead of having the opportunity to yell at the top of his lungs at breakneck speeds on the fastest roller coasters, Carson could only watch. Not by choice. He passionately longed to be the first in line, but the dreaded rules bested him every time. It wasn't like he didn't try to get around them. Along with the help of my wife, he'd try fluffing up his already world-class Afro, wearing his tallest shoes, and even clocking extra hours of sleep on vacation. (Someone told him that a person only grows when he sleeps.) But it was always the same sad story—too short by a few inches!

As we stepped into Sea World that day, there was no confusion—the thrill ride Kraken was calling his name. This time, he told us, it was going to be different.

While I was pulling for my boy (and his hairspray-teased fro), I was secretly nervous for him, for several different reasons. Could he really endure one more day of sitting on the sidelines, watching everyone else have the time of their lives? Were his high hopes just setting him up for a big letdown? Would anyone find out about that growth hormone I had been secretly slipping into his cereal? There was a lot at stake.

We finally made our way to the front of the line, and there it was. The sign. The only thing that lay between Carson and his destiny as a roller coaster veteran.

He walked quickly up to the measuring line on the sign, pausing for the attendant to make the decision.

She suddenly squinted and leaned in closer.

We all held our breath.

Placing her hand on his head, she did what roller coaster attendants always did to Carson: mushed down the fro. *So she's gonna play rough*, I thought.

But it didn't matter. She was just stalling. No hairspray or tissue-stacked shoes needed—he'd done it! Carson was finally tall enough to ride! Humbled, the attendant stepped aside, and he breezed past her, like a prizefighter walking triumphantly out of the ring, sauntering in a slow-motion victory parade with Queen's "We Are the Champions" playing in his head, toward the nearest seat on Kraken.

Carson absolutely loved the ride, but what I remember most about the rest of the day was how he walked confidently up to every other ride. There was no more sweating it out; he had swag and confidence! He would literally call out to the attendants, "Hey, I'm right here—you want to check me? Don't take my word for it. Measure me, I dare you! Go ahead, mush down my fro. I'm ridin' this thing. You just try and stop me!" My little boy wasn't content to just ride these roller coasters; he *owned* them because he knew that he belonged there.

You belong with Jesus out on the water, far from the boat. You were made to let go of the rope and experience the exhilaration of flying through the air. You are His workmanship, and He built you strong, sturdy, and destined for far more than watching while everyone else rides with hands held high.

WHAT IF?

What if you really did it? What if you just pushed play, right now, today?

The truth is, we don't get another shot at this life. And while we always think there will be another time, or a more convenient opportunity to go for it, we *never* know how much time we actually have. Life can get interrupted on a dime and everything can change.

Last fall as I was beginning to work on this book, I began experiencing occasional unexplained pain, but I did what we all do—I pushed through. I figured it would all resolve itself; life was busy, and if things didn't get better, I would get around to taking care of it someday.

At the end of my message one weekend, I became flushed and nauseated. I got offstage in time to lie down and try to get my bearings. No one had to endure the trauma of seeing their pastor throw up mid-sermon, so I thought I had escaped the worst of it.

Nothing could've been further from the truth.

That week I battled a fever that just wouldn't stop. Even visiting the urgent treatment center and dutifully following the doctor's orders didn't help. A week later, I ended up in the emergency room, was admitted, and got transferred to ICU, where a doctor looked at me with unexpected gravity and said things were "serious." I had a substantial infection wreaking havoc in my abdomen, but it wasn't contained there; it had gone septic.

Literally, one day I was preaching about making the most of the life that God has given us, and a week later I was hearing news that was potentially life-threatening.

Thankfully, I had a brilliant team of doctors who developed a great game plan. It took four months of complicated, painstaking daily treatments, countless procedures, and lots of hard work, but I was finally given a clean bill of health.

Friends, you have no idea how much time you have. You don't want to miss the chance to make the one life you've got *count*. I've never been more convinced that I want to seize *every day* I'm given.

What about you? Are you ready to push play? What if you really did it, right now?

What if?

What if you actually decided to go for it and trust Him like you never have before? What might the impact of your life be? In what way will God use you for His glory? To change your city, workplace, neighborhood, family, or marriage? To make the world a better place? What will your life become when you embrace all that the Lord is showing you?

Are you beginning to see it?

Jesus is calling. Only you can decide what happens next.

I can tell you that it will be remarkable, exhilarating, challenging, and fruitful. You will finally become yourself, the person Jesus designed you to be before the beginning of the world. You will impact lives, take risks, and make a difference, all to the glory of God, who crafted you to find out who you are and what you're living for in Him (see Ephesians 1:11, *The Message*).

I pray that you will begin living out all that Jesus has impressed upon you as we've journeyed together. Don't delay. Resist the urge to pause and ponder. Stop waiting—push play and begin living the life you've been waiting for. It starts now.

Jesus is out on the water calling your name. Can you hear Him?

> *Come . . . in the power of My Spirit!*
> Come . . . make war on fear.
> Come . . . leave unforgiveness behind.

Come . . . knowing that I won't drop you.

Come . . . enjoy your Grace Path.

Come . . . embrace who you are in Me.

Come . . . experience My love for you.

Come . . . agree with My work in your life.

Come . . . leave your idols behind.

Come . . . fix your eyes on Me.

Come . . . push play and let our adventure begin.

Jesus is calling. Only you can decide what happens next. What life are you waiting for?

GETTING TRACTION

REWIND

It's always better to be out on the water with Jesus than in the boat without Him.

DOWNLOAD

So Peter went over the side of the boat and walked on the water toward Jesus. MATTHEW 14:29

PUSH PLAY

Make this your heartfelt prayer:
"Jesus, I need Your love and Your power. Help me to trust You as I stop waiting and start living out the Transformation Adventure I was made for. I'm answering Your call. Today I'm pushing play. . . ."

ACKNOWLEDGMENTS

If gratitude is an indicator of the health of a person's heart, then I am a very healthy man. I am deeply indebted to so many people without whom this book would have remained an idea rather than become a reality. I offer my heartfelt thanks . . .

To my family—Jacki, Corey, and Carson, you make me so proud. I never could have hoped for more supportive, impassioned, real partners in this journey. Thank you for loving Jesus and refusing to wait for some other life in which to change the world. You are each a gift straight to my heart from Jesus, and I love each one of you more than I knew I could. Go Team Hise!

To the Quest Staff and Leadership Community—I never saw you coming! You take my breath away!! It is the honor of my life to serve alongside each of you. You are not only exceptional people, you are irrepressible Kingdom advancers. I love every single one of you like family.

To priceless friends—Justin, your tireless work shaping, forming, and praying for this manuscript have been humbling to witness. Your expertise and 24/7 support have been essential. You have served me by helping me capture my voice and continually casting vision for what God just might do through *What Life*.

Sharon, your passion, tears, and constant spurring have helped see me through this long process. God has used you to see "the finished product" for me many times over. Your life is a nonstop reminder of this book's premise. Connie, your heart to serve God by supporting me is humbling. I thank Jesus that He led you to Quest and to me. Dani, Dewayne, Teri, and Angie, you have all helped make this endeavor a real joy, as you do with most things in my life. I love each one of you.

To the Tyndale House team—Your confidence in me and strong support of this message inspired me to give my best and to push through. Jan Long Harris, your wisdom was the final straw that convinced me to push play on this project. Sarah, Bonne, Nancy, Yoli, Sharon, whether editing, marketing, or guiding, I have always felt like I am in capable hands. You have made this first-time author eager for the next assignment.

To the great people God has used in my journey—Bill Hybels, thank you for your investment in me. I can't begin to calculate the impact your mentoring has had on my life and ministry. Clayton King, Steven Furtick, Perry Noble, Derwin Gray, Pete Wilson, Mac Powell, Christine Caine, thanks for cheering me on and helping me see that if God called me to write this book, then He would empower me to do so. God used your collective insight and inspiration at just the right times. I honor each of you. Bob Carlisle, thank you for giving me a soundtrack to inspire and guide my life journey.

To Sealy and the team at Yates & Yates—I am so grateful God brought me to you and led you to take me in. Thanks for your wisdom and advocacy . . . it has been easy to rest in your counsel.

To those who inspired me to keep pushing play—my dad (who finally ran to Him), my sister (who can't believe I wrote a book), Steve (who went first), the Applebee's crew (the forerunners to what is now Quest Community Church), Bill Dean (who got me in the game), Phil (the bass singer for the Christian band Oasis who led me to Jesus—THANK YOU).

Finally, to the One who loved me first . . . who pursued, rescued, and redeemed me from myself; to the One who is Faithful despite my infidelity and True to the end. Jesus, the minute I saw You for who You really are, I ran to You—and You welcomed me like the prodigal who had come to his senses. You ambushed me with Your love and told me who I really am. It is the prayer of my heart that I might bring You honor and fame for the rest of my life. I am Yours. Use me . . .

ABOUT THE AUTHOR

PETE HISE is the founding and lead pastor of Quest Community Church in Lexington, Kentucky. Growing up in New York, Pete radically encountered Christ on November 12, 1982, and was thoroughly redeemed by the love of Jesus. Since May 1999, Pete's compelling teaching, consummate leadership, and authentic relational evangelism have shaped the culture of redemption at Quest, embodied in its mission of "transforming unconvinced people into wholehearted followers of Jesus."

Pete holds a master of divinity degree from Asbury Theological Seminary and a BA in religion and philosophy from Houghton College. As a featured speaker at the Ichthus Festival, Christian and Missionary Alliance General Council, Asbury Theological Seminary, Asbury University, and The Uprising, Quest's annual church leadership experience, Pete most relishes speaking to and challenging the local church. He and his wife, Jacki, have two sons, Corey and Carson, and make their home in Lexington, Kentucky.

BRING
WHAT LIFE ARE YOU WAITING FOR?
INTO THE LIFE
OF YOUR CHURCH!

Visit http://whatlifebook.com today for **FREE**
resources including videos, downloads, a small group
discussion guide, and more!